# Teens Dodging
# "Bullets"

*Equipping Teens to Survive Mass
Shootings, Bullying, Suicide, and More*

## Michele Sfakianos, RN, BSN

Teens Dodging "Bullets"
Equipping Teens to Survive Mass Shootings, Bullying, Suicide, and More

Open Pages Publishing, LLC
http://www.my411books.com
(239) 454-7700

ISBN: (e) 978-1-7322722-0-0
ISBN: (sc) 978-0-9960687-9-6

Library of Congress Control Number: 2018941287

Because of the dynamic nature of the Internet, any Web addresses or links contained in
this book may have changed since publication and may no longer be valid. The views
expressed in this work are solely those of the author and do not necessarily reflect the
views of the publisher, and the publisher hereby disclaims any responsibility for them.

Website: http://www.my411books.com

Disclaimer

The information in this book is:

- of a general nature and not intended to address the specific
  circumstances of a particular individual or entity;
- not gender specific; you will find instances where he/him/
  his is mentioned, but they can also refer to she/her/hers;
- written as a guide and is not intended to be a comprehensive tool, but
  it is complete, accurate, and up to date at the time of writing;
- intended as an informational tool and not intended to be used in place of a visit,
  consultation, or advice from a medical, legal, spiritual or other type of professional.

This book is not intended to serve as professional tax or legal advice. If you need
specific advice, you should always consult a suitably qualified professional.

*This book is dedicated to the teens who have lost their lives due to senseless school shootings, peer pressure, bullying, suicide and so much more.*

# Table of Contents

# Preface

Our evening news is full of stories. Crimes committed by teens are on the rise. Crimes such as school shootings, bullying, car invasions, burglaries and many others. What has our world come to? We are sending our kids to school with backpacks and tablet covers that are bulletproof. How did we get here?

The pressure on our teenagers is too much for many of them to handle. The teen years are a time of confusion and upheaval for both teens and parents. This is due to intense physical and intellectual growth.

How do you feel when you hear about a teenager struggling to fit in who decides to give up on life and commits suicide? I want to be able to send this message to our youth: "Everybody's different, and it's OK." Some teens develop early, some late, and other teens are slow but steady. In other words, there is a wide range of what's considered *normal*.

Preadolescent children between the ages of 10-13 are "tweens." Tweens are more advanced in their social skills. This is due to exposure of "adult content" much earlier in life than in previous years.

The primary goal of the teen years is to achieve independence. For this to occur, teens will start pulling away from their parents. They will pull away from the parent they are closest to first. Teens are between the sweet innocence of childhood and the responsible maturity of adulthood. Although capable of making decisions, many teens are not ready for the change.

Adults struggle with the tween and teen years. This is due to the importance of parental involvement. We know kids don't want to be shielded from the realities of life and tough choices. Yet, we still want to protect them the best we can. How easy or difficult the transition will be, depends on your parenting style and how you were raised.

I remember when my children went through the tween and teen years. It seemed so different from what I had experienced. Most parents face, or have faced, this situation as well. Times change. People change. Situations change. But the love for a child never changes. This is the reason why it is hard for parents to let go. Now more than ever, it is important for parents to get involved in their kids' lives. Parents need to ask the hard questions. We need to encourage our children to answer these questions without harsh consequences.

It is my goal to inform teens and parents about the obstacles faced during teenhood and how to survive them. If both tweens/teens and parents understand the journey, perhaps the outcome will be positive. What is normal for one, is not the normal for all. We need to be able to recognize when our kids are in trouble and be ready to act on it.

I no longer want the word *teenager* to be something people dread or fear. I want everyone to look forward to those years with hope and understanding.

Although I wrote this book for parents, I encourage both teens and tweens to read the entire book. It's important for all to understand each other's feelings and what is "normal."

# Acknowledgements

Thank you to everyone who has supported my writing. If it weren't for your faith in me, I would not have been challenged to write more self-help books. I know the long hours of research and fact checking were totally worth the time and effort so that I might enlighten the lives of others.

Thank you to my parents for being there for me during my teenage years. Thank you to my husband and children for their love and support. My family has been a vital part and huge inspiration for writing the series. Providing the information to everyone, through our experiences, has been rewarding.

It is my hope that this book will help to save lives. Join me in the fight to save our children and future generations.

# Introduction

When I say the word teenager what comes to mind? If you are like most people, the words *rebellion, trouble,* and *stubborn* come to mind. You might also think:

- School shootings
- Drugs
- Crime
- Pregnancy
- Peer pressure
- Sex
- Puberty
- Driving
- Attitudes
- Relationships
- Irresponsible
- Messy

Those about to go through the teen years might think:

- Independence
- First job
- Fun
- Sports
- Adventure
- Dating
- Invincible
- Driving

What is a tween? A tween is a preadolescent child between the ages of 10 and 13. What is a teenager? A teenager is a person between 13 and

19 years old. These individuals are between the protection of childhood and the responsibility of adulthood. The teen years are also known as the adolescent years. Don't confuse puberty and adolescence. Puberty has visible signs such as breasts, menstrual periods, pubic hair, and facial hair. But, there are also invisible signs. These invisible changes are preadolescence and adolescence.

Those nights leading up to turning thirteen and becoming a teenager can be exhausting. For years, he was a kid - your child. Your new teen now wants to know if he is supposed to automatically look or feel different. He will wonder if he will enter the cool set of teens in the neighborhood—the teenhood. He or she will realize every piece of clothing is critical and will wonder what others think about him or her. Believe it or not, your teen may wonder if you will still love, approve of, and accept him or her. Teens may want to explore dangerous things, painful things, silly things, and illegal things. What about school? Teens will point out those who have not completed their studies. They will wonder if they should keep up their own standards or follow other's behaviors.

Compared to prior generations, our teens are in need of more protection. It is far more difficult to protect today's teens from dangers presented to them. They experience stresses younger children do not face, such as sex, drugs, and violence. Yet teens do not have to shoulder the responsibility of adulthood such as jobs, bills, and family. Are our teens struggling by having to grow up too fast? How prepared are they to take on adult responsibilities? This is why we must take action.

At this stage in life, teens are responsible for their choices. Yet, parents are in part, to blame when a teen makes a mistake. People will make quick assessments of teens when they make mistakes. People will also make a quick assessment of a teen by their appearance. Appearance can serve as a clue to a teen's character and upbringing. It can be confusing when the most colorful dressers come from good families. Appearance may also signal:

- whether your teen is a troublemaker;
- what type of work ethic he or she has;
- if there is parental involvement; and
- whether they have solid morals or values.

Today there is a general, but limited, acceptance of a teen's unique appearance. This offers an opportunity to define a youth's unusual style as individual. It can also be viewed as positive exploration and a harmless search for identity.

Communication is important in the teenage years. Are we talking too much about "back in our day" when we should be listening to what's happening in our kid's day? Your teen may begin to pull away from you. This should not take away from the fact that he or she still needs direction and discipline. Even the most responsible teen will still need help from his or her parents or caregivers. Your teenager may not be able to express the need for help. Make sure to watch for clues, which we will discuss later. The most important part of communication is being able to hear what *isn't* being said.

It is time to change the way adults see teenagers. Teens today face horrible violence, drugs, teen pregnancy, and other dangers. Why do our teens use drugs and alcohol? Gamble? Fall prey to other destructive behaviors such as eating disorders or cutting? Why do they think it's OK to kill another individual? What are they dealing with that is so bad that they self-destruct? Why do we think it's someone else's responsibility to fix our kids?

We will walk through these and other scenarios, and I will offer guidance on how to get through it.

Throughout the book I will refer to "teens" but the information applies to our tweens as well.

We take our children through childhood, into teenhood, and then onto adulthood. Remember: if you go into the adventure together, you will come out of it together.

# 1

# Growth and Development

O ur tweens and teens will go through physical, mental, social, and emotional changes. The biggest change is puberty, or the process of sexual maturing. It happens between the ages of ten and fourteen for girls, and ages twelve and sixteen for boys. The changes in the body (hormonal changes) can sometimes be confusing, depending on the age. Since the teen years are defined as between the ages of thirteen and nineteen years old, if the body begins changing before that, they may feel different from other kids the same age. What is normal for one person can be different for another, and that's OK!

## Physical Changes

Girls:

- Girls may begin to develop breast buds as early as eight years old. Breasts develop fully between ages twelve and eighteen.
- Girls have a rapid growth in height between ages nine and fourteen, peaking around age twelve.
- Pubic hair, armpit and leg hair begin to grow at about age nine or ten and reach adult patterns at about thirteen to fourteen years old.
- The beginning of menstrual periods (menarche) typically occurs about two years after early breast development and the first appearance of pubic hair. It may occur as early as age ten, or as late as age fifteen. The average age of menstruation is about twelve years old.

Boys:

- Boys may begin to notice their testicles and scrotum grows as early as age nine. Soon after, the penis begins to lengthen. By age sixteen or seventeen, their genitals reach their adult size and shape.
- Boys' voices change at the same time as the penis grows. Nocturnal emissions, or wet dreams, occur with the peak of the height spurt.
- Pubic hair, armpit, leg, chest, and facial hair growth begins at about age twelve and reaches adult patterns at about fifteen or sixteen years.
- Boys do not start puberty with a sudden incident, like the beginning of menstrual periods in girls. Having regular nocturnal emissions, or wet dreams, marks the beginning of puberty in boys. These nocturnal emissions start between ages thirteen and seventeen, with the average at about fourteen years.

## Emotional and Social Changes

The emotional and social changes of teenagers will vary from teen to teen, but the majority of them will experience the following:

- Concerns about body image, looks, and clothes
- A focus on themselves; going back and forth between high expectations and lack of confidence
- Increased moodiness
- More interest in the opposite sex
- A deeper capacity for caring, sharing, and for developing more intimate relationships
- Feel stress from more challenging schoolwork
- May develop eating problems
- Show more interest in, and influence by, a peer group
- Express less affection toward parents; sometimes might seem rude or short-tempered
- Spend less time with parents and more time with friends

- Feel sadness or depression, which can lead to poor grades at school, alcohol or drug use, unsafe sex, and other problems.

## Thinking and Learning Changes

- Teens will learn more defined work habits.
- They will show more concern about future school and work plans.
- They will be better able to give reasons for their choices, including what is right or wrong.
- They will have more ability for complex thought.
- They will be better able to express feelings through talking.

Normal growth and development is supported by good nutrition, adequate sleep, and regular exercise. Despite data collected for growth and development charts, normal heights and weights are difficult to define. Growth patterns, in most cases, are determined by genetics. Shorter parents may tend to have shorter kids, and taller parents may have taller kids.

It is normal for girls to be critical of their weight. But doing so can sometimes lead to unhealthy body image concerns and dieting practices. Boys tend to be more concerned with their height and muscle development, but this can also lead to unhealthy practices, like using steroids and protein supplements. Teens worry about being different from their peers and about anything that causes them to feel like they don't fit in with others or don't feel normal. Take your concerns to your physician. Your doctor can provide reassurance that other kids have the same concerns about their size as your child does.

## Discipline

We are all thankful when our child ages out of the toddler tantrums, but the tantrums aren't over yet. You now have the teen terror and teen mean. The teen years aren't unlike toddlerhood; your teen will test his boundaries. Adolescents thrive on the balance of caring and positive discipline. Teens have difficulty respecting a parent's authority.

Suggestions on discipline:

- Set clear rules and put them in writing.
- Go easy on first offenses. Remember, you were a teen once.
- Talk about it. Verbal communication is an important aspect of discipline.
- Avoid hands-on discipline. Discipline should always be lighter for teenagers than for younger children. Allow consequences to be as natural as possible. Let them demonstrate what he or she learned.
- Do not scold. Voicing disapproval does not work. Teens are not dumb. Teenagers know what will happen if they do not study or do whatever is required of them. Show your child the respect of letting him make his own decisions, and live with the consequences as long as no one is in physical danger.
- Be firm and consistent. Teens are master manipulators.
- Take away cell phones, iPods, iPads, and other communication devices for a specified period of time.

Before you come down hard on your teen for misbehaving, try to understand what's driving the action. Could there be trouble in school, with a boyfriend or girlfriend, or bullying? Get your kids to open up to you about their problems by creating an environment of honesty and respect. Let them know you're always available to talk about anything. Even sensitive subjects like sex and drug use shouldn't be off-limits. Let your teens know you will always love and support them, no matter what.

## Temptations

Kids are exposed to the temptations of sex, drugs, and alcohol everywhere, at all ages. By the time your child is thirteen, he may have decided whether to become involved with chemical substances. Sex rears its head early, too. As your teenager evolves, it may shock you what he is like, what he is into, and to what he is exposed. Get familiar with what is out there. Know the risks and the dangers.

Here are the realities:

- Adolescence is a time of stress, and, yes, your teen may be awful and cruel sometimes.
- Adolescents can be charming, warm, caring, and interesting. It is a joy to watch them come into their own selves.
- Teenagers do not want an adversarial relationship any more than parents do.
- Rebellion is a trait of a teenager, and your teen isn't any more messed up than other teenagers.
- What matters is not the structure of the family but the quality of it.

We will further discuss teenage temptations in coming chapters.

# 2

# Nutrition

Eating healthy can sometimes be tough. After all, most teens are busier and busier with school, sports, part-time jobs, and other activities. What kids eat is not always high on the priority list. For teens on the go, nutrition consists of whatever they can eat in the car, racing between activities. While the ill effects may not show now, poor nutritional habits will catch up to them. In fact, teens may show the effects of less than desirable nutrition practices now and are unaware of it.

## Poor Nutrition

The US Food and Drug Administration places emphasis on iron and calcium because of the special roles these nutrients play in teen development. Lack of iron can lead to anemia and sluggish feelings during the day, affecting alertness in school, at work, and even during athletic participation. Iron intake is important for teenage girls, as menstruation depletes iron. Calcium is important for future health. Brittle bones in the future can lead to osteoporosis and other health problems as a result of a lack of calcium during the teen years.

The effects of regularly eating junk food, such as fast food, soda, potato chips, and other popular snacks, include the following:

- Increased risk of heart disease
- Increased tendency toward hypertension, a.k.a. high blood pressure
- Increased risk for diabetes later in life
- Onset of sleeping disorders, such as apnea

- Risk of becoming obese, now or later in life
- Some cancers are related to excess fat and sugar intake
- Increased risk of psychological problems associated with negative body image.

## Proper Nutrition

Nutrition is based on individual needs. How many calories your teen should consume depends on their activity level. Teen boys need between 2,200 and 3,200 calories a day to keep up with the growing demands of their bodies. The more active a teenage boy is, the more calories he needs. Teen girls need fewer calories, 1,800 to 2,400, each day. Again, her activity level will indicate whether she needs to consume a higher number of calories.

Teens require ample fruits and vegetables as well as an appropriate amount of low-fat dairy products. Protein is abundant in meat, fish, and poultry. Iron is found in dark green vegetables such as broccoli and spinach. Calcium comes from dairy products, which also provides protein. Sources of fiber include whole grain breads, cereals, and fruit.

Teen vegetarians can still get adequate nutrition. Calcium sources include calcium sulfate-processed tofu, leafy green vegetables, soymilk, and orange juice fortified with calcium. High-iron vegetables include: broccoli, spinach, watermelon, and raisins. Vegans should take a vitamin B-12 supplement, although soymilk has the same fortification.

Eating the proper nutrients does not have to be a terrible task. There are naturally sweet foods that taste good. Portable snacks include:

- Baby carrots
- Dried fruit
- String cheese
- Wasabi peas
- Apple or orange slices
- Nuts, unsalted

## Obesity

Experts point out a sedentary lifestyle and poor nutrition choices have contributed to the growing number of teens considered overweight or obese. Factors contributing to a teen's unhealthy weight gain include:

- Increased intake of junk food, such as fast food, chips, cookies, and other sweets
- Drinking sugary drinks, especially soda
- Lack of physical activity, including our schools' decisions to cut physical education classes
- Temptation of indoor sedentary activities including television, video games, and computer use
- Genetic factors

Sixty-one percent of parents claim they would change their own habits if it would help their teenagers avoid obesity. Hence, one of the main means of preventing obesity: family involvement. It is important for your teen to allow the family to help him or her acquire healthy lifestyles through family activities and participation. Concentrating on replacing unhealthy foods with healthy food choices can significantly reduce obesity, as can increased physical activity. Family activities such as walking, biking, hiking, and even playing games outside can help everyone lower their risk of obesity.

One of the biggest culprits in teen obesity: sugary drinks. Non-diet sodas, canned juices, lemonades, sweet iced tea, and other similar beverages have large amounts of calories. According to research published in the Journal of Pediatrics, cutting back on sugary drinks and replacing them with low-calorie alternatives (especially water) can have a significant impact on preventing weight gain.

Your teen doesn't have to participate in organized sports or forgo all sweets and snacks to avoid obesity. Teens can get creative and watch TV while walking on a treadmill or play video games while riding a stationary bike. They can take a brisk walk for thirty minutes each day.

Snacks like peanut butter on celery or apple slices are healthy choices, as is a trail mix of raisins, dried fruits, unsalted nuts, and a few M&Ms or chocolate chips. Just take into consideration that snacks, along with other foods, should be consumed in moderation and be included in calorie counts.

There are ways to avoid obesity. You and your teen must to be willing to take the extra steps.

## Eating Disorders

The three main types of teen eating disorders are:

- Anorexia nervosa, also referred to simply as anorexia
- Bulimia nervosa, also known as bulimarexia or simply bulimia
- Binge eating disorder, also known as binge eating or binging

The National Eating Disorders Association (NEDA) identifies several categories of factors that can lead to eating disorders:

- Emotional: People who binge-eat may identify particular emotions, including anger, sorrow, boredom, and worry, that can lead them to binge.
- Psychological: Depression can be associated with a binge eating disorder. More than half of patients have a history of major depression. Low self-esteem has also been cited as connected.
- Interpersonal: Interpersonal factors contributing to eating disorders are a history of problematic family or personal relationships, trouble expressing emotions, and/or a history of either physical or sexual abuse.
- Social/cultural: Media images have a strong effect on body image, particularly for women, because the ideals the media presents for women are farther from the average woman's body.

## Anorexia Nervosa

Anorexia, means without appetite, and nervosa refers to the nervous system. Although anorexia is associated with teenage girls, it is not limited to this gender.

People with anorexia are called anorectics. Because anorectics consistently deprive their bodies of needed nutrition in the form of calories, vitamins, electrolytes—fluids with nutrients—and other nutrients for long periods of time, a number of complications can arise.

Complications of anorexia include:

- Heart problems, including heart failure
- Malnutrition
- Kidney problems, including kidney failure
- Amenorrhea, or cessation of menstruation
- Muscle atrophy
- Osteoporosis
- Death

Treatments for anorexia include:

- Nutrition counseling to provide helpful guidelines for healthy choices
- Medical intervention to address issues created by malnutrition, electrolyte imbalance, endocrine issues, and other medical complications
- Psychological counseling, including the family and teen

## Bulimia Nervosa

Bulimia Nervosa, also referred to as bulimarexia or bulimia, comes from the words "ox" and "hunger," referring to the enlarged appetite characterized by it. Research tells us between 2 and 3 percent of teens have a form of bulimia.

Bulimia has two parts. The first part of bulimia includes binging or uncontrolled overeating. The second involves unhealthy behaviors, such as fasting; purging, which may include vomiting; using laxatives, or using diuretics, also known as water pills; and/or over-exercising. Another bulimic practice includes chewing food and then spitting it out without swallowing.

The teen with bulimia may not show the dramatic weight loss seen in people with anorexia. They may appear to be healthy, although they are not. Bulimia has a strong association with the feeling of being out of control.

People who have bulimia are called bulimics. Because the behaviors of bulimics involve overeating and methods of purging, which occur repeatedly over a long period of time, a number of complications can arise, such as:

- Heart problems, including heart failure
- Tooth decay
- Ulcers and pancreatitis
- Electrolyte imbalance (not have a normal amount of sodium or potassium)
- Irritation and other damage to the throat and esophagus
- Laxative addiction- or laxative-use related damage to the kidneys or colon
- Stomach problems, including rupture of the stomach
- Death

Bulimia tends to run in families. It may result from a combination of factors, both genetic and environmental. It may also be linked to depression and obsessive compulsive disorder (OCD).

As with other eating disorders, the treatment for bulimia may include:

- Nutrition education
- Behavioral adjustment, including eating, purging, and exercising behaviors

- Resolution of interpersonal issues
- Addressing mood issues, such as depression or anxiety

## Binge Eating Disorder

Binge eating disorder, also known as binge eating or binging, is a disorder in its own right, as well as one of the major symptoms of bulimia. On its own, it is sometimes referred to as BED. It includes uncontrolled overeating without any of the other secondary behaviors. Those with BED have a feeling of being unable to control one's own eating. People who binge-eat may identify particular emotions including anger, sorrow, boredom, and worry, which can lead them to binge.

Binge eating, which is the first part of bulimia, includes the following:

- Eating alone due to embarrassment
- Eating unusually large amounts of food, though people who are healthy may do this periodically and have no disorder
- Eating particularly fast
- Eating when not hungry
- Eating past the point of comfortable fullness
- Experiencing negative feelings after overeating
- Gaining weight

People who have binge eating disorder are called binge eaters. Because of the behaviors of binge eaters involve overeating over a long period of time, a number of complications can arise, such as:

- Type 2 diabetes
- High cholesterol
- High blood pressure
- Gall bladder disease
- Heart disease

Depression can be associated with a binge eating disorder. More than half of patients have a history of major depression. Low self-esteem has also been cited as connected.

Binge eating disorder is treated with various approaches. These approaches are designed to address the underlying causes, make changes in behavior and relationships, and to help create and sustain healing.

Other treatments include:

- Changes in eating behavior and habits
- Addressing body image
- Interpersonal therapy to address relationships
- Medication therapy to address depression

If your teen exhibits behaviors associated with an eating disorder, get professional help.

# 3

# Acne and Other Skin Conditions

The teen years are a time of skin breakouts, and many teens feel singled out when it comes to skin conditions. But the truth is that skin problems are common to all teens. I understand these times can be embarrassing, but it is important to remind them they are not in the situation alone. It is a fact of life, and there are treatments available. You need to find the right treatment for your teen.

## Acne

As hormone levels rise and bodies change, stress kicks in and skin reacts. Genetics can also play a role in the appearance of acne. If other people in the family have or had acne, your teen may be more likely to develop it, too. The average teen suffers an occasional pimple or blemish. For girls, it can occur right before menstruation. For others, breakouts go far beyond the pimple or two, creating a chronic condition known as acne, which is characterized by whiteheads, blackheads, and pus-filled pimples.

Contrary to what you may have heard, acne is not caused by dirty skin. It is caused by overactive oil glands in the skin and an accumulation of oil, dead skin cells, and bacteria, which leads to inflammation in pores.

Although there is no way to prevent acne, try these tips to help reduce the number and severity of breakouts:

- Washing skin is essential, as it helps remove excess surface oils and dead skin cells, which can clog pores. But washing too much can cause damage by over-drying the skin or irritating existing acne.

- Wash after exercising, because sweat can clog pores, making acne worse. If your teen works around greasy food or oil or has been sweating, from heat or because of working hard, have them wash his or her face and other acne-prone areas as soon as possible.
- If your child uses skin products, such as lotions or makeup, use ones labeled "noncomedogenic" or "nonacnegenic," which means the product won't clog or block pores.
- Keep hairspray or styling gel away from the face as much as possible. Some hair products contain oils, which make acne worse. Try to use water-based products.
- If your teen gets acne on areas such as the chest or back, avoid wearing tight clothes, which can rub and cause irritation.

Treatment for acne will consist of multiple therapies. The key may be to purchase several products and rotate them.

- Over-the-counter acne treatments containing benzoyl peroxide or salicylic acid
- Various acids in a cream, lotion, or gel
- Professional-strength acne products prescribed by a primary care practitioner or dermatologist
- Antibiotics
- Special laser or other light treatments
- Abrasive therapies

It may be tempting to squeeze or pop pimples, but doing so will not get rid of the problem. Squeezing can push infected material and pus further into the skin, which can lead to more swelling and redness, and even scarring, which can be permanent.

Eating nutritious food can help to keep your teen healthy, and his or her skin will benefit from getting enough vitamins and minerals. But the bottom line is that you don't need to be obsessive about what your teen eats or how often she washes her face to control acne. If you do not find an over-the-counter product that works well, talk to your doctor or dermatologist for advice on living through the acne years.

## Oily Skin

Although oily skin and acne go hand-in-hand, it doesn't happen with everyone. A number of teens suffer from oily skin alone. If his complexion is oily, but he's not breaking out, there are two treatment approaches.

1.  Use topical treatments to "soak up" the oil. Use products containing alcohol, such as a drying solution, to soak up excess oil on the surface of the skin. You can also use blotting products, sheets of specially treated paper you dab on the face, to absorb oil.
2.  To get to the root of the problem, which is excess oil production, and to stop it completely will involve using professional laser treatments. These treatments interact with the oil glands to make them less active. The treatment will last from months to one year.

What you don't want your teen to do is wash his or her face excessively, trying to get rid of the oil. Doing so strips the fatty oils from the skin and is more harmful than beneficial. Instead, use a gentle cleanser and wash no more than twice a day.

## Excessive Sweating

If you often find your teen drenched in perspiration or sweat, be it on the palms of their hands, soles of their feet, under the arms, in the scalp, or anywhere on their body, they are not alone. Excessive sweating is a major issue for teens.

Sweating can result from two conditions:

1.  Stress can cause excess sweating, most often occurring under the arms.

2.  When heavy sweating occurs on a regular basis, your teen may
    have what doctors call hyperhidrosis. The characteristics of
    hyperhidrosis include excessive sweating on the palms, soles,
    and underarms, and sometimes the face.

Treatment for the first condition requires a maximum-strength
antiperspirant. If the over-the-counter antiperspirants do not help, your
doctor can prescribe medical-strength products.

Treatments for the second condition include minimally invasive surgical
treatments to target the sweat glands, as well as Botox, the same
substance used as a wrinkle treatment for adults. The treatment lasts
up to eight months and can be repeated.

Tips to control excess sweating are:

- Wear natural fibers like cotton, which are cooler and absorb
  sweat.
- Use absorbent inner soles, and try to alternate shoes. Allow
  shoes to dry before wearing again.
- Avoid foods and drinks that seem to trigger sweating. These
  are different for everybody, but experts say it may include spicy
  dishes or hot liquids such as soups.

For the most severe cases of hyperhidrosis, doctors can perform surgery
on the nerve bundles that control sweating. It is a specialized surgery
available at major medical centers.

## Warts

Warts are flesh-colored, or sometimes dark, lumps and bumps that grow
under fingernails, on fingers, on the backs of hands, or on the soles of
the feet. A virus causes warts and impacts mostly teens.

The treatments available for warts:

- Freeze the growths with liquid nitrogen
- Burning them off with a laser
- Chemical treatment

Although treatments can work, warts can return. The best ways to avoid warts:

- Avoid biting the nails.
- Avoid injuring the hands.
- Don't touch warts or pick at existing warts.
- Protect cuts and scrapes.
- Wear shoes.

Injured skin appears to be more susceptible to the wart virus. Most warts go away without treatment within two years or so. Warts are not dangerous. If your teen is disturbed by warts, your primary health care provider can discuss various treatment options with you.

## Eczema/Atopic Dermatitis

Although more common in younger children, these patches of dry, scaly, reddened skin can follow kids into their teens. Teens involved in sports find their childhood eczema grows worse when aggravated by trauma or by sporting equipment worn on the knees or ankles.

Most times, a non-perfumed, heavy-duty moisturizer is all you need. This is particularly important if you shower after sports or go out into cold weather, which can further dry and irritate skin. Your teen should apply the moisturizing lotion immediately after showering, bathing, or swimming.

If he or she does not get relief from the moisturizer, and the skin begins "weeping," oozing, or becomes significantly red or itchy, see a dermatologist, who can prescribe medications to help.

# 4

# Sleep Disorders

S leep is food for the brain. Important body functions and brain activity occur during sleep. Skipping sleep can be harmful, even deadly, particularly if one is behind the wheel. Sleepiness can make it hard to get along with others, can hurt scores on school exams, and can have an effect on the court or on the field performance. Remember: a brain hungry for sleep will get it, even when you don't expect it. For example, drowsiness and falling asleep at the wheel causes more than 100,000 car crashes each year.

Sleep is vital to your teens overall well-being, as important as the air they breathe, the water they drink, and the food they eat. It can even help your child eat better and manage the stress of being a teen. Biological sleep patterns shift toward later times for both sleeping and waking during adolescence, meaning it is natural to not be able to fall asleep before eleven o'clock. Most teens need about eight and a half to nine hours of sleep each night in order to function optimally. The majority of teens do not get enough sleep. Teens tend to have irregular sleep patterns throughout the week, typically staying up late and sleeping in late on the weekends, which can affect their biological clocks and hurt the quality of their sleep. Many teens suffer from treatable sleep disorders, such as narcolepsy, insomnia, restless legs syndrome, or sleep apnea.

Not getting enough sleep may:

- limit the ability to learn, listen, concentrate, and solve problems. It even can cause your teen to forget important information like names, numbers, homework, or a date with a special person in their life;

- make the teen more prone to pimples. Lack of sleep can contribute to acne and other skin problems;
- lead to aggressive or inappropriate behavior, such as yelling at friends and being impatient with teachers or family members;
- cause overeating or lead to unhealthy food choices, like sweets and fried foods, which can result in weight gain;
- heighten the effects of alcohol and possibly increase use of caffeine and nicotine;
- contribute to illness;
- cause the teen not use equipment safely;
- cause the teen to drive while drowsy.

## Prevention

- Make sleep a priority. Decide what you or your teen needs to change in order for him or her to get enough sleep to stay healthy, happy, and smart.
- Naps can help pick your teen up and make him or her work more efficiently—if you plan them right. Naps too long or too close to bedtime can interfere with regular sleep.
- Keep your teen's room cool, quiet, and dark. If you need to, buy eyeshades or blackout curtains. Let in bright light in the morning to signal the body to awaken.
- No pills, vitamins, or drinks can replace restful sleep. Consuming caffeine close to bedtime can impair sleep, so your teen should avoid coffee, tea, soda, and chocolate late in the day in order to sleep at night. Nicotine and alcohol also interfere with sleep.
- Don't allow your teen to leave homework for the last minute. Try to avoid the TV, computer, and telephone in the hour before bed.
- Sleep deprivation has the same impairment as driving with a blood alcohol content of .08 percent, which is illegal for drivers in certain states. Drowsy driving causes over 100,000 crashes

each year. Make sure your teen can recognize sleep deprivation, and encourage him or her to call someone else for a ride.

- Establish a bedtime and wake-time pattern and stick to it, coming as close as you can on the weekends. A consistent sleep schedule will help your teen feel less tired since it allows the body to get in sync with its natural patterns. You will find it easier for him or her to fall asleep at bedtime with a routine.
- Have your teen do the same things every night before going to sleep in order to teach the body the signal of bedtime. For example, have your teen take a bath or shower to help him or her relax. This could also free up extra time in the morning.

Most teens experience changes in their sleep schedules. Their internal body clocks cause them to fall asleep and wake up later. It is hard to change the habit, so you must find what works best for your teen. Make sure activities at night are calming in order to counteract the already heightened alertness.

## Narcolepsy

People with narcolepsy are often sleepy during the day. They are prone to sleep attacks, which cause them to suddenly fall asleep, lose muscle control, or see vivid, dreamlike images while dozing off or waking. Someone's nighttime sleep may be disrupted by frequent awakenings throughout the night.

Narcolepsy can be dangerous because people fall asleep without warning, making it hazardous to do things like drive. The unusual sleep patterns affect a narcoleptic's school, work, and social life.

Narcolepsy is not commonly diagnosed in teens and cases often go unrecognized. People first begin to have symptoms between the ages of ten and twenty-five, but they may not be properly diagnosed until ten to fifteen years later. Doctors treat narcolepsy with medications and lifestyle changes.

## Insomnia

Lots of people have insomnia, or trouble falling or staying asleep. The most common cause of insomnia is stress. But all sorts of things can lead to insomnia, including physical discomfort, like the stuffy nose of a cold or the pain of a headache; emotional troubles, like family problems or relationship difficulties; and even an uncomfortable sleeping environment caused by a room that is too hot, cold, or noisy.

It's common for everyone to experience insomnia from time to time. But if it lasts for a month or longer with no relief, then doctors consider it *chronic*. Chronic insomnia can be caused by a number of problems, including medical conditions, mental-health problems, medication side effects, or substance abuse. People with chronic insomnia can often get help for their condition from a doctor, therapist, or other counselor.

## Sleep Apnea

A person with a sleep apnea disorder temporarily stops breathing during sleep because the airway becomes narrowed or blocked. One common cause of obstructive sleep apnea is enlarged tonsils or adenoids. Tonsils and adenoids are tissues situated in the area connecting the nose and throat. Being overweight or obese can also lead a person to develop obstructive sleep apnea.

People with obstructive sleep apnea may snore, have difficulty breathing, and even sweat heavily during sleep. Because it disrupts sleep, someone with sleep apnea may feel extremely sleepy or irritable during the day. A doctor should evaluate people who show signs of obstructive sleep apnea, such as loud snoring or excessive daytime sleepiness.

Treatment for sleep apnea may include:

- Change in lifestyle, such as losing weight.

- Continuous Positive Airway Pressure (CPAP)-a machine that delivers air pressure through a mask placed over the nose during sleep.
- Expiratory Positive Airway Pressure (EPAP)-small single-use devices placed over each nostril before you go to sleep.
- Oral appliances designed to keep your throat open.
- Surgery

## Restless Legs Syndrome and Periodic Limb Movement Disorder

People with restless legs syndrome (RLS) feel physical sensations in their limbs, such as tingling, itching, cramping, or burning. Teens with RLS can relieve these feelings by moving their legs or arms to get rid of the discomfort.

People with periodic limb movement disorder (PLMD) have involuntary twitches or jerks. The involuntary movements are due to the person's inability to consciously control them, and they are often unaware of the movements.

Doctors can treat PLMD and RLS. For some groups of people, treating an iron deficiency can make them go away; other people may need to take other types of medication.

## Nightmares

Most teens have nightmares on occasion. But frequent nightmares can disrupt sleep patterns by waking someone during the night. Certain things can trigger frequent nightmares, including certain medications, drugs, or alcohol. Sleep deprivation can also be a cause.

The most common triggers for more frequent nightmares are emotional, such as stress or anxiety. If the nightmares interfere with your teen's sleep, talk to a doctor or counselor.

# 5

# Peer Groups

As your children enter into teenhood, they are discovering their likes and dislikes as well as what works best and what doesn't. Another obstacle teens face is how they fit in with others. There will always be new social groups forming. Most teens find people they like and stick with them, and others try new things—not necessarily the right things—to try to fit in. The issue is what will your teen try in order to fit in? Will your teen fall prey to the social games of today?

## Sample Peer Groups

Here is a list of the peer groups teens often fall into:

- Cool kids: This is your classic teen stereotype—otherwise known as rebellious, disobedient, and/or reckless—basically, everything you would expect a teen to be.
- Jocks/Cheerleaders: Every school has them—guys and girls whose lives revolve around team sports. These teens hang together, have their special language, talk strategy, and project an image of elitism.
- Dealers: The drug dealers/users are generally the nicest guys/girls in the school. Although most don't perform well grade-wise, as far as overall likeability goes, these teens get along well with all groups.
- Geek/Nerds: Stereotypical nerds are thin, spotty, and wear glasses. Modern-day nerds often look normal but are pale from extended periods in libraries and laboratories. These teens are super-smart and love to engage in academic discussions.

- Goth: They wear black makeup, black hair, and black clothes. Most have several areas of body piercings.
- Drama Queens: These teens overemphasize everything, and to them, nothing is ordinary. A broken nail is a total disaster and a missed ride, a tragedy. Their dramas are accompanied by expansive gestures and loud monologues.
- Emos: Short for emotional, these teens are into deep feelings and are known by their dress code. Tight black jeans and T-shirts, studded belts, and black hair worn long over one eye are sure signs of an emo. Similar in appearance to Goth.
- Gangsters: A group of adolescents who associate closely, often exclusively, for social reasons, including engaging in delinquent behavior. A gangster is a member of a criminal gang, which means a group of teens who possibly commit crimes.

There are teens that do not associate themselves with groups and prefer to hang with one or two friends instead. A teen may have difficulty interacting with others if she didn't see her parents interact with their friends. The fear of rejection by others can be hard to face.

## Are Peer Groups Healthy?

Peer groups can divide society as a whole. Some teens that belong to a group will identify themselves with the group rather than identify with what makes them an individual. Other teens can belong to a group and still know their identity. Today we have various technologies to send messages to others by way of social media outlets. We can make some of the people, who we would never include before, now feel included. Teens will "friend" people through the social media site Facebook in order to have lots of *friends*, not because they *are* their friends. Peer groups, therefore, can be both healthy and unhealthy.

Teach your teens that the car they drive, the home they live in, and the people they hang out with do not define who they are. *They* define who they are. Let your teen know that the choices they make in life will label them but not define them.

*Do you know your kids friends?*

## Games Kids Play

Kids just want to fit in. Many will try to take part in the games of today without knowing the end result. Being the most unpredictable of all age groups, teens are experimenting with the new online and social games. Children who play these games are often driven to self-injury, sharing explicit photos online and even suicide. Parents may think that their children would never take part in these games but sometimes the lure is too strong to ignore. Social pressure takes precedence over what's rational. A simple trigger can prove disastrous, and even fatal.

Here are 20 of the most popular games:

1. **Choking game.** This game involves strangulation by using a noose or strap to cut off the oxygen supply to the brain and create a high. A CDC study noted 82 reported choking game deaths found those who died ranged in age from 6 to 19, with the average age being 13 years old. Most who died were playing alone.

2. **Cinnamon challenge.** This game made headlines after being seen on YouTube®. Someone swallows a teaspoon full of cinnamon, which immediately dries out the mouth. The painful effects may include violent coughing and vomiting. The cinnamon can also enter the lungs and require respirator-breathing support.

3. **Knockout challenge.** This is another asphyxiation game. A teen inhales and exhales rapidly, causing hyperventilation. Another youth then presses against his or her chest to inhibit air flow, causing the child to lose consciousness.

4.  **Car surfing.** A teen surfs on top of a moving car's hood, roof or trunk. According to the CDC, nearly 100 teens have died from this game in the past 18 years.

5.  **Chubby bunny.** Players put as many marshmallows in their mouth as they can and try to utter the words "chubby bunny." Some have choked while playing.

6.  **30-second fight game.** Kids brawl violently for 30 seconds, causing potentially serious injuries. Onlookers watch the fight and declare a winner at the end.

7.  **ABC games.** Using a fingernail, something sharp or even a pencil eraser (this is also known as the eraser game), one person digs at another youth's skin while they list words beginning with each letter of the alphabet. The skin breaks but the game continues until the child either gives up or finishes the alphabet game.

8.  **Sack-tapping**. Similar to an old game involving punching someone in the arm until they give up, this game targets the testicles. It has led to permanent injuries, in some cases requiring surgical removal of one or both testicles.

9.  **Robotripping**. A kid chugs a full bottle of cough syrup. The syrup produces a high induced from the chemical DXM (dextromethorphan), which in large doses can produce hallucinations and can kill in excessive amounts. More than one in 10 teens has used over-the-counter cough or cold medicines to get high, according to the Drug Enforcement Agency.

10. **Gallon challenge**. In this game, a child drinks a gallon of water or milk within a one-hour period. The human stomach can't handle this volume, so the person becomes violently ill, vomits and may suffer diarrhea and cramps.

11. **Ice and salt challenge.** In this game, the skin is moistened, salt is added and then ice is applied. This causes severe pain until the player gives up. The result can include severe skin damage from frostbite.

12. **Skittling.** This life-threatening game consists of grabbing pills from the medicine cabinet, mixing them up and swallowing a small and random handful of them.

13. **Kylie Lip Challenge.** This challenge involves grabbing a shot glass and putting your lips inside it and then sucking as hard as you can. It artificially plumps your lips and the results are startling and dangerous. Experts say the shot glass can break under the pressure, resulting in broken blood vessels, requiring stitches, and other issues when undergoing this challenge.

14. **The Condom Challenge.** Fill a condom with water like a balloon and tie the end, then one teen drops the condom on another teen's head while recording the entire thing. While some of the results are funny, at least to teens, condoms are not balloons and this challenge has led to hospitalizations.

15. **The Eye-Balling Challenge.** Teens take a shot of hard liquor... into their eye socket. This can cause cornea scarring, swelling, irritation, and plenty of other issues.

16. **Vampire Biting.** Teens are taking the vampire movie rage too far by actually biting one another like a modern-day hickey. There are plenty of risks from these bites such as infection, scarring, HIV, hepatitis, and more.

17. **The Snorting Challenge.** Teens are challenging one another to snort a variety of objects into their nose and pull it out their mouths. Items used include condoms, balloons, string, and plenty of other objects. This can lead to serious damage, choking, and death.

18. **The Cold-Water Challenge.** This challenge is similar to the ice bucket challenge (which was created to raise awareness for the ALS Association,) but it has its differences. Instead of dumping water over their heads, teens jump into cold bodies of water. Submerging into cold water can lead to hypothermia and other illnesses. One teen in Minnesota did the challenge alone and ended up drowning.

19. **The Fire Challenge.** Instead of using water, some teens are moving in the opposite direction. Teens put flammable liquid on themselves and then light a match. Hazards are obvious and range from serious second and third-degree burns, and death.

20. **The Ghost Pepper Challenge.** These peppers, also called Bhut jolokia, are the hottest in the world. Teens stick the pepper in their mouths and record their reactions. This leads to excruciating pain in the mouth, but some people also get worse reactions. It can cause nausea, vomiting, and a trip to the hospital.

And – last but not least – and the most disturbing game is **The Blue Whale Challenge.** A game spread over 50 days, the Blue Whale Challenge instructs the participant to complete 50 tasks that include self-harm, watching scary videos, waking at odds hours, etc. As the game progresses with each task, the participant reaches the final day that builds up to suicide. The person must prove that they have completed the tasks by sending proof – such as pictures – to their 'curator' or the 'whale', the one who had been instructing them through the challenge. As of 2017, the challenge has claimed over 130 deaths.

No parent can prevent every accident. But, every teen can avoid falling prey to any of these challenges by simply realizing how dangerous they can become in a matter of seconds. Talk about these games openly, without judgment, so everyone is well informed.

# 6

# Computer Usage and Cyberbullying

Since almost every household has a computer today, I am sure you are already familiar with the basics. Computers, both desktops and laptops, are expensive. It is important for you to teach proper care and use. I cannot stress how important it is to purchase a spyware and antivirus program. If you get a virus on your computer, it can completely erase your hard drive and all of your information will be gone. If your computer isn't protected, someone could hack into it and steal personal information you may have stored. Do not make yourself vulnerable to these attacks. Make sure your teen knows the basics.

## Computer Basics

- Use a surge protector.
- Unplug electrical equipment during a lightning storm. Even the best surge protector cannot block a lightning strike.
- Do not click on e-mail attachments you are not expecting, especially if you do not know the sender.
- Do not fall for phishing schemes. No one will get rich quick, and the person from Nigeria, or other foreign country, will not send millions. Teens can fall prey to these scams as well. Make sure your teen is aware of them.
- When you have a computer problem, look for the obvious first. Always make sure the device is plugged in and all cables are attached.
- When all else fails, power off and restart the system.

- If the power goes off, unplug the system. When power is restored, there are surges and spikes that can damage your equipment. Plug the computer back in after the power is restored.
- To clean the keyboard, turn the system off, turn the keyboard upside down, and shake to remove crumbs. You also can use a spray device from a computer store to clean it.
- Wipe the dust gently from the screen. Do not press hard on a laptop screen, as it can cause permanent damage.
- Do not give personal information to anyone in a chat room.
- Limit the personal information you provide on social media sites.
- Make sure to set your security settings on your social media sites. Do not let anyone you don't know view your information.
- If you use a wireless router, make sure to password protect it. If you do not, your neighbor can use your wireless device and possibly hack into your computer.
- If you use Wi-Fi at a local coffee house or restaurant, shield the laptop screen from the wandering eyes around you.
- Install a spyware and antivirus software program to protect your computer from hackers and viruses.
- When purchasing something online, input personal information only on those web pages that are secure and locked. You will see a padlock somewhere on the site that will indicate the site is safe. If you do not see a lock, don't enter personal information especially credit card numbers.
- When all else fails, contact customer support for your product.

It is a known fact that teenagers use the Internet better than adults and are likely to hide their online behaviors from them. It is important now more than ever to know what parental controls are available, and you can password protect the controls. If you decide these controls are not necessary, at least know your teen's online passwords and monitor their activity.

## What Is Cyberbullying?

Mean kids have been around forever, but today's technology has given them a whole new platform for their actions. Years ago we heard, "sticks and stones may break my bones, but words can never hurt me." This no longer holds true. Virtual name-calling can have real-world effects on teens.

Cyberbullying is the use of technology to harass, threaten, embarrass, blackmail, or target another person. Although it occurs among young people, adults have taken part in these actions as well. When an adult is involved, it may meet the definition of cyber-harassment or cyber-stalking, which are crimes with legal consequences and involve jail time.

Cyberbullying can also happen by accident. One teen's joke or sense of humor could be another's devastating insult. Either way, repeated patterns of e-mails, text messages, and online posts are rarely accidental.

At times cyberbullying can be clear-cut. For example, if a teen leaves overtly cruel cell phone text messages or mean notes posted to websites, this is intentional and is considered cyberbullying. Other times the acts are less obvious, such as impersonating a person online or posting personal information or videos designed to hurt and embarrass them.

## How Does Cyberbullying Differ from Other Bullying?

New technologies have created new outlets for bullying.

Today cyberbullying:

- can take place 24/7, not only during school hours;
- provides evidence such as e-mails, texts, photos, or videos, in a way other forms of bullying doesn't;
- invades your home and personal space as well as the school environment;

- can be done quickly and on a large scale because of the speed and reach of e-mail, mobile devices, and websites;
- can last longer than face-to-face bullying, sometimes building over weeks and months;
- can be perceived as anonymous. The bully can set up a fake email address or use someone else's mobile;
- means bystanders can become perpetrators if they pass on emails or text/picture messages or take part in an online discussion;
- incidents may be unintentional or a joke, and the perpetrator might not have considered the potential consequences.

## What Are the Signs of a Cyberbully?

If your teen is a victim of cyberbullying, please contact your local law enforcement agency. Do not allow others to make your teen feel ashamed for who they are. Your son or daughter cannot be afraid of computer privileges being jeopardized by telling you something has happened.

Look for these signs that your teen is a victim of cyberbullying:

- Signs of emotional distress during or after using the Internet
- Hesitant to be online; nervous when an email, text message, or instant message appears
- Avoids school or group gatherings
- Slipping grades and acting out in anger at others
- Withdrawal from friends or activities
- Hides or clears the computer screen or closes the cellphone when you enter the room
- Changes in mood, behavior, sleep, or appetite

## Effects of Cyberbullying

Severe cyberbullying can leave victims at greater risk for:

- Anxiety
- Depression

- Undermining confidence, self-esteem, and sense of security
- Affecting performance and attendance at school
- Causing stress and affecting health
- Affecting professional reputation and career
- Fueling prejudice in areas such as race, religion, and sexuality
- Affecting the victim for the rest of his or her life
- Suicide

If you or anyone you know is a victim of cyberbullying, please get help.

## Is His or Her Friend a Cyberbully?

Getting bullied by a close friend is more common than most people know. Part of loving someone is the ability to put up with his or her changes in personality. But oftentimes a person becomes too tolerant. What is a friend? A friend is someone who has a kind personality, will do anything for anyone, and who people think highly of. It is not OK for a friend to put another person down, call him names, or tell him that he doesn't fit in. A person displaying this behavior is not a friend, so make sure your teen knows to stop acting as if they are.

If you think a bully is a big guy at school who steals lunch money, you only have part of the story. The truth is that girls often bully their friends through text messages. Teen girls put up with terrible behavior from their friends because they keep calling them friends.

At times we relax our boundaries and allow people we love to make us feel small because we love them, or we fear we can't find someone better. In these situations, losing the relationship feels more painful than staying in it. But, wouldn't it be better to find someone to accept your teen for who she is and not want to change her? We should all be able to give and receive constructive criticism from a true friend. Encourage your teen to find a friend who has the courage to tell her things face-to-face and not a coward who resorts to cruel text messages and emails.

## Why Do People Cyberbully?

- It's anonymous: The web lets you hide behind a fake user name or alias, and bullies feel protected by their *false identity*. Because these individuals feel hidden and shielded, bullies might do and say things they would never dream of doing or saying to someone face-to-face.
- Revenge: If a person is bullied in school, he might decide to fight back online. You don't have to be a typical bully to be cruel with instant messaging or e-mail. Teens savvy with technology see online cruelty as a way of getting even with people who push them around in the real world.
- Others do it: Being mean or hurtful online may seem like something kids do—simply a part of life. A person may see his or her friends do it and think it is OK. Sometimes online bullies start out small, with a funny comment or joke. Then things get out of hand. They start posting meaner and meaner things, and before they know it, they're hurting people with the things they write.

## What Can You Do?

People who get dumped by boyfriends or girlfriends need to play the field and meet new people; the same thing is true when you need to make a new friend. Help your teen find situations where he will meet new people. Encourage him to join a new club or team, sit down at a new lunch table, try a new partner on a project, and chat with or text a new person he wants to get to know better. It's not always easy, and sometimes you get friends that don't work out, just like real dates. But sometimes teens click, and it's awesome.

More tips for talking to your teens about cyberbullying:

- Don't go to websites you know are unsafe or are favorite hangouts for bullies.

- Never share private or personal information with someone you don't know or don't trust.
- Never post your e-mail address on a public message board or in a chat room. E-mail is for people you know and trust.
- Never post a comment or send an e-mail when you're angry.

If someone is mean to your teen online, don't retaliate. Everything inside of you will want to get back at them. By retaliating, it will allow the bullying to keep going. Ignore it. Face-to-face, it can be hard to walk away from an insult. Online, it's much easier. Encourage your teen to turn off the computer and walk away. Instruct her not go back to websites or chat rooms where she's been bullied. If your teen is bullied through e-mail, block the senders e-mail address or ISP address. If you don't know how to block, ask an expert to help. Report the incidents to local law enforcement. The person doing the bullying may be on a watch list. They made need serious help. Don't just look the other way and hope someone else will step up.

# 7

# Shoplifting

A child understands the concept of stealing by the age of seven. When your child reaches teenhood, she knows stealing is wrong. Do you know if your teen has shoplifted?

Teen shoplifting is one of those things that may be difficult to detect. Research shows teenage shoplifting is not limited to troubled teens with problems. And shoplifting is an equal-opportunity crime. Both males and females from all different socio-economic backgrounds steal. While teen shoplifting can be a sign of a troubled teen, it can also be a problem for teenagers with few issues beyond the typical behavior of a growing teen.

## Why Do Teens Shoplift?

Reasons for stealing can differ from teen to teen, and any one teen will steal for a number of reasons, such as:

- Poor impulse control and need for instant gratification
- To draw attention to themselves
- A lack of family closeness and feelings of neglect; in some cases a stolen object might serve as a substitute for love
- The thrill or the thought of getting away with it
- Suffering a form of abuse and need help
- Expressing displaced feelings of anxiety, anger, or alienation as a result of a major life change, such as parental separation or divorce, moving to a new school, or being rejected by peers
- Revenge for the pain others have inflicted on them. They steal to get even or to hurt someone

- Crave what others have, but they cannot afford; wanting to keep up with the latest styles
- Want to fit in with a peer group who steals
- Need money to buy drugs

## What if Your Teen Is Caught?

If your teen is caught stealing, the first thing to do is remain calm. *Yeah, right.* You want them to be aware that there are consequences for their actions, but you don't want to show your anger. Do not humiliate them; find out the reason why. You will need to take them back to the store and ask for the store manager and/or the security personnel. Most stores do not prosecute the first time it happens, and most judges, depending on the state, are fairly lenient on first-time offenders. You, the store, and the judge should make your teen aware that the consequences increase with each offense.

Take time to ask yourself why the behavior occurred. You will want to determine:

- whether your teen has a specific problem or issue;
- whether your teen is seeking attention;
- which of the reasons listed above fit your teen.

## Selling Stolen Items

With the rise in technology and social media websites, teens sell stolen items over the Internet. Most teens believe they cannot get caught because no one knows who they are. This is where they're wrong. Websites have investigators working in direct contact with retailers in order to connect stolen items through UPC codes, or other codes, from items people sell online. Getting caught is tough enough for teens and their families, but what's also at stake is a moral standard.

## Kleptomania

Adults and teens both can suffer from kleptomania, or an addiction to stealing items not related to personal use or a monetary gain. There may be no underlying reason for teenage shoplifting by someone with kleptomania. In such cases, professional help is often needed to help treat this mental health disorder. Kleptomania may be accompanied by other personality or eating disorders.

## Get Help

You will need to get help for your teen if she or he has issues with theft. Teens who refuse to stop stealing will develop other self-destructive habits. Once a teen is in the legal system, he faces tougher future treatment. Many states have revised their codes so that records aren't always wiped clean at age eighteen, like in the past, and Internet databases mean even minor convictions may stick. A teen with a legal record can have difficulty getting into college, earning scholarships, and finding work.

# 8

# Self-Mutilation and Injury

## What Is Self-Mutilation?

Self-mutilation—sometimes called self-injury, self-harm, self-abuse, or self-inflicted violence (SIV)—means inflicting deliberate harm to one's own body without the intent to commit suicide. Currently there are five identified elements common to all self-injury behaviors:

1. The injury is done to the self.
2. The individual inflicts the injury.
3. It involves physical violence.
4. The injury is intentional.
5. There is no conscious intent to commit suicide.

Self-mutilation is a negative way to deal with strong emotions. Self-mutilation behaviors include:

- Ripping or picking the skin
- Hair pulling
- Punching
- Head banging
- Bruising
- Burning
- Branding
- Scratching
- Bone breaking

Among teens, the most common, and perhaps the least noticeable, self-mutilation behaviors tend to be skin picking and hair pulling.

According to an article from http://www.cnn.com "One in five teens states they have purposely injured themselves at some time."

## Who Is at Risk for Self-Mutilation?

Recent studies suggest girls and boys are equal in the number of those who self-mutilate. Those who engage in SIV often have been victims of physical or sexual abuse, have an alcoholic parent, have a substance abuse problem, have an eating disorder, or suffer from another mental condition, like bipolar or obsessive-compulsive disorder.

Teens who self-mutilate often display these characteristics:

- Low self-esteem
- Difficulty controlling impulses
- High anxiety levels
- Difficulty coping with stressful situations
- A tendency to hide away in their own space for hours on end

## Why Do Teens Self-Mutilate?

Teens engage in self-harm for various reasons, such as:

- Mental health problems, like depression, anxiety, or obsessive compulsive disorder (OCD)
- To release tension
- To relieve feelings of emptiness
- To punish themselves
- To express anger or other unacceptable feelings
- To have control or to feel alive
- To stop bad thoughts
- To calm themselves
- Wanting to get the attention of people who can help them
- To feel euphoric—a mental and emotional condition in which a person experiences intense feelings of well-being, elation, happiness, ecstasy, excitement, and joy

Self-injury can work as a coping mechanism to help teens release tension, relieve stress, and overcome feelings of depression. These behaviors can be used like a drug, to provide temporary relief from pain or other overwhelming feelings the teen can't otherwise deal with. And like drugs, SIV can even be habit forming.

Teens who lack the skills or maturity to verbally express their feelings may demonstrate their emotions through self-mutilation. These teens also lack healthier physical outlets, like involvement in sports or engaging in exercise, to release tension or deal with strong emotions.

## Signs of Self-Mutilation

Self-injury often goes undetected because teenagers are ashamed of the behavior and often go to extreme lengths to prevent parents, family members, and even close friends from discovering their secret.

Here are common signs of self-harm. If you observe these, you should investigate further.

- Evidence that your teenager's friends self-mutilate.
- Your teen regularly locks himself away for long periods in his room or the bathroom.
- Your teen exhibits a loss of interest in usual friends or social activities.
- You find sharp objects hidden in her room or other strange places.
- Your teen has a history of eating disorders.
- You notice the appearance of an abnormal number of injuries or scars.
- Your teen begins wearing long sleeves, even in hot weather.

Self-injury or self-mutilation can often be addictive and can become increasingly serious. It is possible for teens to stop self-injury or self-mutilation, but it requires professional help. If you know or suspect your teen is self-mutilating, or you know someone who is, please tell someone and get help. Self-mutilation can be deadly.

## Intermittent Explosive Disorder (IED)

Intermittent explosive disorder is characterized by repeated episodes of aggressive, violent behavior in which one reacts grossly out of proportion to a situation. Road rage, domestic abuse, and angry outbursts, or temper tantrums involving throwing or breaking objects, may be signs of intermittent explosive disorder (IED).

People with intermittent explosive disorder may attack others and their possessions, causing bodily injury and property damage. These explosive eruptions may last ten to twenty minutes and often result in injuries and the deliberate destruction of property. Afterward, people with intermittent explosive disorder may feel remorse, regret, or embarrassment.

Nearly two-thirds of American teenagers admit to having anger attacks that involve destruction of property and/or threatening or engaging in violence. One in twelve has intermittent explosive disorder, and people often continue to have problems into adulthood, which can affect their education, jobs, and marriages.

Aggressive episodes may be preceded or accompanied by:

- Irritability
- Increased energy
- Rage
- Tingling/Tremors
- Palpitations/Chest tightness
- Headache or a feeling of pressure in the head

The cause of intermittent explosive disorder is unknown, but the disorder may be caused by a number of environmental and biological factors. Most people with IED grew up in families where explosive behavior and verbal or physical abuse were common. Being exposed to violence at an early age increases the likelihood that their children will exhibit the same traits as they mature. There may also be a genetic component, where the disorder is passed down from parents to children. Higher levels of the hormone testosterone have been associated with intermittent explosive disorder.

Factors that can increase the risk of developing intermittent explosive disorder are:

- having another mental health problem. Teens with other mental illnesses, such as mood or anxiety disorders, may be more likely to also have intermittent explosive disorder;
- having a history of substance abuse. Teens who abuse drugs or alcohol have an increased risk of intermittent explosive disorder;
- age. Intermittent explosive disorder is most common in the teens and early twenties;
- being male. Men are far more likely to have intermittent explosive disorder than women;
- having a history of physical abuse. Teens abused as children have an increased risk of intermittent explosive disorder.

The violent behavior that is part of intermittent explosive disorder is not always directed at others. People with IED are at a significant increased risk of harming themselves, either with intentional injuries or suicide attempts. Those who also are addicted to drugs or have another serious mental disorder, such as depression, are at the greatest risk of harming themselves.

Others often perceive teens with intermittent explosive disorder as always appearing angry. Other complications of intermittent explosive disorder may include job loss, school suspension, auto accidents, or incarceration.

## Treatment for IED

Although IED is listed in the *American Psychiatric Association's Diagnostic and Statistical Manual*, the cause and how best to treat it remain unknown. There's no one treatment that is best for everyone who has intermittent explosive disorder. Treatment generally includes medication and individual or group therapy.

There are several types of drugs used to help control intermittent explosive disorder, including:

- Antidepressants
- Anticonvulsants
- Anti-anxiety agents
- Mood regulators

Individual or group therapy sessions can help. A commonly used type of therapy, cognitive behavioral therapy, helps people with intermittent explosive disorder identify situations or behaviors that may trigger an aggressive response. More important, cognitive behavioral therapy teaches people with intermittent explosive disorder how to manage their anger and how to control their inappropriate response by using relaxation exercises.

## Coping and Support

If your teen recognizes his behavior in the description of intermittent explosive disorder, talk with your doctor about what treatments are available for him, or ask for a referral to a mental health professional.

Coping is a learned behavior. Have your teen write down what happens before the episode and how he feels afterward. Cognitive behavioral therapy or anger management will help him recognize what pushes his buttons and how to respond in ways that work for him instead of against him. Teens need to learn to remove themselves from a situation when they experience the feeling of losing control.

Oftentimes, people with intermittent explosive disorder don't seek treatment. If you suspect that someone you love has intermittent explosive disorder, it's important for you take steps to protect yourself and others. If you see a situation is escalating, and you suspect your teen may be on the verge of an explosive episode, try to safely remove yourself and anyone else from the area.

In an emergency, call 911—or your local emergency number—or your local law enforcement agency. The episodes are not your fault. The key is to keep everyone safe and seek help. We can no longer look the other way and hope things will get better. Our kids are in trouble and need us to help them. That's what unconditional love is all about.

# 9

# Dating and Dating Abuse

As we move into the adolescent years, dating is a hot topic around everyone's home. It's normal for a teen to be interested in dating. Girls become more vocal about their dating interest at a younger age, but boys are definitely taking notice. School dances and parties present dating opportunities, although most of these activities do not require a date.

As parents, it is our job to make sure our teens are prepared. Teens whose parents talk to them about dating are better prepared and much happier. While the topic of teens and dating can make even the most confident parents nervous, you should do your best not to project those anxious feelings when discussing dating, including when you discuss the rules and limitations. By talking about what you expect of them during a date, it may also help to alleviate the unknown of what should or shouldn't be expected during a date.

A teen does not learn how to date in school and most likely has picked up on some of the basics, like respecting someone's personal space, at home. If their friends are already dating, they will learn from them and not necessarily the things you want them to know. It is important you and your teen set, and agree to, the rules of dating.

## Having the Talk

Before your teen is asked out on a date, you should talk to them about how he or she feels about dating. Don't tiptoe around the subject. It's important to get everything out in the open, even if things feel uncomfortable. Your role as a parent now changes, and all change feels awkward at first.

Things to discuss:

- What is an appropriate dating age?
- How will they get to and from the date?
- What age group is acceptable for them to date?
- How will they pay for the date?
- What is their definition of personal space?
- How long should the date last?
- What time is their curfew?
- Should there be a chaperone? Many cultures require a chaperone.
- How long should they know the person before going on the date?
- What type of person do they seek? (Common friends and/or interests, or something completely different.)

When you talk with your teen, set up certain scenarios—"what happens if"—as teens are notorious for getting themselves into situations they cannot easily escape. You need to let them know you are always available for a ride home. You will pick them up anywhere, no matter the time of day or night, without questions or consequences, because you want them to be safe.

## Dating Abuse

The Centers for Disease Control (CDC) reported that nearly one in ten teens in grades seven to twelve, both male and female, have been physically abused by a boyfriend or girlfriend. Abused teens are more likely to drink alcohol, use drugs, engage in risky sexual behavior, develop eating disorders, and attempt suicide.

People can experience many types of abuse, including:

- physical abuse, which is an intentional use of physical force meant to cause fear or injury;
- emotional abuse, which includes non-physical behavior such as threats, insults, humiliation, stalking, intimidation, or isolation;
- sexual abuse, which is when someone forces undesired sexual behavior on you, such as making you do anything you don't want to do sexually, refusing to have safe sex, aggressively pressuring you to go further than you are comfortable with, or making you feel bad about yourself sexually.

Your teen should be aware of the warning signs of an abusive relationship and how to tell if he or she is a victim of teen dating violence. These include:

- Sexual pressure
- Any form of physical violence
- Controlling behaviors
- A partner threatening to hurt others or him/herself
- Jealousy

Other warning signs to watch for if you suspect your teen is in an abusive relationship:

- Alcohol or drug use
- Unexplained injuries
- Changes in appearance
- Apologizing for a partner's behavior
- Jealousy or possessiveness
- One partner insults, embarrasses, or criticizes the other
- Changes in behavior or mood
- Withdraws from friends and family
- Receiving too many text messages from his or her partner

"Abuse will continue over time, and will become more serious, leading to death in approximately 1,300 cases each year," according to the CDC. It is important to not judge your teen if you suspect abuse. Be supportive and make it clear the abuse is not her fault. You should encourage your teen to stay out of contact with the abuser. If you know the abuser, do not attack him, but make it clear the behavior is not acceptable and will not be tolerated. Contact local law enforcement to report the abuse. Obtain a restraining order, if necessary, to keep the abuser away.

## Date Rape

Teen date rape is a widespread crime. Sexual intercourse—vaginal, anal, or oral—is rape if the teen did not want it. Date rape also occurs if a teen agrees to one type of sexual contact but is forced to perform other sexual acts.

Talking to your teen about date rape can be difficult, but you must do it. Rape is not always avoidable, so your teen needs to know what can be done to reduce the risk of being a date rape victim. Date rape drugs are often used to rape teens. The drugs have no smell, taste, or color and can be added to your teen's drink without her knowing. Most date rape drugs will leave your teen helpless—unable to move, see, or escape.

To avoid being a victim of date rape, teach your teen the following:

- Trust your instincts; if you don't feel comfortable with a person or a situation, leave.
- Always carry a cell phone, phone card, or money to call someone to help you get out of a situation.
- Learn how to defend yourself.
- Stay in control; don't drink or use drugs and don't get in a car with someone you don't know well.
- When you have a drink, do not set your drink down or leave it unattended. If you do, throw it away when you return.
- Go to a party in a group. Try not to do things alone.
- If a person is forcing you to do something you don't want, be loud and forcefully tell him or her *NO* and get away. Making noise can attract help and scare a would-be attacker.

Discuss these procedures with your teen in the event they become a victim of date rape:

- Leave the area without touching anything and go to an emergency room or the nearest police station immediately.
- Do not shower, wash, urinate, or change clothes.
- Prepare to be examined by nurses and doctors. The staff will record the injuries and check for evidence that can be used against the attacker.
- The doctors and nurses will treat your injuries and check you for sexually transmitted diseases, which can be spread even if your attacker used a condom or forced you into oral or anal intercourse.

Date rape and dating abuse causes emotional harm, including feelings of guilt, depression, anger, worthlessness, distrust, and insomnia. It can also cause difficulty with normal sexual relations later in life. Victims should seek counseling to help them heal from the emotional damage. Professionals also recommend that victims join a support group. Free counseling is available to rape victims in most areas.

If someone you know has been a victim of date rape or dating abuse, listen and offer comfort. Help the person get medical care and counseling and reinforce the fact that it is not the victim's fault.

# 10

# Cell Phones: Life Saving and Life Threatening

Today it's not a matter of *whether* a teen will own a phone, but *when* a teen will own a phone. Cell phones have come a long way. You can text, take and send pictures, record videos, play games, listen to music, track people's locations, surf the Internet, and so much more. Along with cell phones comes great responsibility. Parents have given their teens cell phones for emergency purposes and have forgotten to put restrictions on the usage. Text messaging and sexting is popular with the younger teens now, so it is important to limit what your teen can do on his or her cell phone.

## Sexting

Sexting is the act of sending sexually explicit messages or photographs, primarily between cell phones. Sexting that involves a minor who sends an explicit photograph of himself to others has led to a legal gray area in the United States. Teenagers who have texted photographs of themselves, or of their friends or partners, have been charged with distribution of child pornography, while those who have received the images have been charged with possession of child pornography; in some cases, the possession charge has been applied to school administrators who have investigated sexting incidents as well.

Talk with your teen and explain what should be considered before pressing "send."

- Don't assume anything you send or post on social media will remain private. Messages and photos get passed around, even if you think they were sent in private.
- There are no "take backs" from cyberspace. Anything you post or send will never truly go away. Potential employers, college recruiters, teachers, coaches, friends, enemies, parents, or strangers may find past posts, even if you think you have deleted them. Even if you have second thoughts about your post and delete it, you have no idea who has already copied and reposted it. It is important to remember that even if someone only knows your screen name, online profile, or email address, anyone can find you.
- Never give into the pressure of doing something uncomfortable. For teen girls, pressure from guys is the reason they send and post sexually suggestive messages and photos. For guys, pressure from friends is why they post sexually suggestive messages and photos.
- Consider the reaction of those receiving the text or photo. Although a message is meant to be fun, it doesn't mean the person who gets it will see it as fun. It's easy to be more provocative or outgoing online, but whatever you write, post, or send will contribute to the real-life impression you make.

It is important when you purchase a cell phone to review the parental block options available. Set these parental blocks ahead of time, and let your teen know what capability comes with his or her new phone. Be prepared, as you *will* meet resistance. You may also save them a lifetime of embarrassment should they decide to send certain personal photos to others.

If you don't feel parental blocks are necessary, you may want to go through your teen's phone periodically to make sure he isn't compromising his future. Research studies have proven that parents who monitor cell phone usage have teens with a lower likelihood of sexting and/or regretting a text message.

Most teens prefer to text than to talk on the phone. The studies are inconclusive as to whether this has an effect on their social abilities to communicate. Most think it is an added layer of communication.

Today, many parents have adopted a cell phone usage contract that both the parents and teens sign and abide by. (See Appendix A) If the rules are broken, it is not a surprise that you take the phone away as a punishment.

## Health Risks

Teenagers who excessively use their cell phones are more prone to disrupted sleep, restlessness, stress, and fatigue. Addiction to cell phones has become so common that teens rely on their cell phones to boost their moods. Teens feel pressure to remain connected and reachable around the clock. When not in contact with others, teens can become restless and agitated.

Children start to use mobile phones at an early stage of their life. There's a connection between intensive use of cell phones and health-compromising behavior, such as smoking and use of alcohol or drugs. Other issues that are of concern are attention and cognitive problems. Therefore, it is best to limit cell phone usage to certain hours. Like computers, cell phones are considered a stimulant and should not be used within an hour of bedtime.

# 11

# Drug, Alcohol, and Substance Use

A t this point, you may think there aren't enough hours in the day to have all of the talks necessary for every circumstance your teen may face. I want to emphasize these are not one-time, ten-minute conversations but ongoing daily discussions, as certain situations arise. These are called *teachable moments*. You could be driving down the road and see teens smoking at a bus stop. Use this time to point out the serious, harmful effects smoking can have on the body, especially over a long period of time. Please understand that scare tactics won't work. You can't tell kids not to do something because they will get cancer, heart failure, or another type of disease. Most kids (and adults) think they are invincible and have an "it will never happen to me" attitude. It happens more than you think, which is why it is important to keep open lines of communication with your children, starting at an early age. Look for those teachable moments every chance you get. Make sure to explain TV commercials and sitcoms. You don't get to drive off in a fast car if you smoke a cigarette, you won't look sexy if you drink an alcoholic beverage, and those things that look glamorous on TV can ruin your life.

Substance use among teens ranges from experimentation to dependence. The consequences range from none to minor to life threatening, depending on the substance and frequency of use. Even minor use raises the risk of significant harm, including overdose, motor vehicle accidents, and consequences of sexual contact, such as pregnancy and sexually transmitted diseases. Parental attitudes and the examples parents set regarding their own use of alcohol, tobacco, prescription drugs, and other substances are a powerful influence.

There are reasons our teens use drugs, drink alcohol, or engage in other substance use. Here are reasons why our teens may become addicted:

- Peer pressure
- Family pressure
- Push to succeed
- Stress
- Shame
- Identity issues
- Family dysfunction
- Feelings of emptiness or discontent

## Alcohol

Alcohol is used most often by teens and is a major factor in teen motor vehicle accidents, homicides, suicides, and drownings. Society and media portray drinking as acceptable and even glamorous. Aside from these influences, parents can make a difference by outlining clear expectations in regards to drinking, setting limits consistently, and monitoring. Teens whose family members are heavy drinkers may think the behavior is acceptable. A number of teens who try alcohol go on to develop an alcohol abuse or dependence disorder. Risk factors for developing a disorder include starting to drink alcohol at a young age and genetics. You should make your teen aware of the increased risk if you have a family member who has an alcohol-dependence disorder.

Binge drinking, consumption of four or more drinks on a single occasion within the past two weeks, is a major problem on our college campuses. It is binge drinking, as opposed to drinking in general, that causes most of the alcohol-associated harm that occurs on campuses and in students' lives. Despite efforts to curb binge drinking on college campuses through alcohol-prevention programs, there is still more work to be done. Education has to begin at home, and the sooner the better.

## Tobacco

The majority of adults who smoke cigarettes started smoking during their teenage years. Children as young as age ten experiment with cigarettes. If teens do not try cigarettes before age nineteen, they are unlikely to become smokers as adults.

These are risk factors that will increase the likelihood of a teen smoking:

- Parents who smoke
- Peers who smoke
- Role models or celebrities who smoke

Risk factors often associated with smoking include:

- Poor school performance
- High-risk behavior, such as excessive dieting, physical fighting, use of alcohol or drugs
- Poor problem-solving abilities
- Poor self-esteem
- Poor nutrition
- Poor hygiene

You can help prevent your teen from smoking by:

- being a positive role model and not smoking;
- having open discussions about the hazards of tobacco.

If they are already smoking, encourage them to quit. Seek medical help, if necessary, to begin the process of quitting.

## Drugs

The Office of National Drug Control Policy has compiled a database of more than 2,300 street terms referring to specific drug types or drug activity. What a scary number. Because of all of the assorted names associated with street drugs, teens may have no idea what they are experimenting with.

While there has been a marked decrease in the use of some illegal drugs like cocaine, data from the National Survey on Drug Use and Health (NSDUH) show that nearly one-third of people aged twelve and over who used drugs for the first time in 2009 began by using a prescription drug non-medically. There has been a notable increase in the misuse of prescription drugs, such as narcotic pain drugs, anti-anxiety drugs, and stimulants. Teens use over-the-counter (OTC) cough and cold drugs to get high. Although these drugs are widely available, most department stores have a system in place to prevent teens from purchasing them. Since the OTC drugs are considered safe, these drugs also serve as starter drugs. Teens will try drugs as young as age twelve.

Would you know if your teen uses drugs? Signs to look out for:

- A sudden change in friends
- Decrease in school performance
- Loss of interest in sports or hobbies that were enjoyable before
- Depression, mood swings, or withdrawal from society
- Erratic or unpredictable behavior
- The discovery of drugs or drug paraphernalia

## Other Substance Use

Listed below are samples of household products that can be used as drugs:

- Glue
- Lighter fluid
- Cleaning fluids
- Spray paint
- Bath salts
- Nail polish remover
- Hair spray

- Gasoline
- Air conditioner fluid, also known as Freon
- Correction fluid

Inhalants are used in various ways. These products are sniffed, snorted, bagged (fumes are inhaled from a plastic bag), or huffed (inhalant-soaked rag, sock, or roll of toilet paper in the mouth) to achieve a high. Inhalants also can be sniffed straight from the container. You may think the effects are not as serious as other drugs, but they are. Most inhalants produce a rapid high that resembles alcohol intoxication. If sufficient amounts are inhaled, users have a loss of sensation, and even a loss of consciousness. Irreversible effects can result in hearing loss, limb spasms, central nervous system or brain damage, or bone marrow damage. Sniffing high concentrations of inhalants may result in death from heart failure or suffocation as inhalants displace oxygen in the lungs. The user can also suffer from *Sudden Sniffing Death Syndrome*, meaning the user can die the first, tenth, or hundredth time he or she uses an inhalant. The scariest part about the addiction is its accessibility. All these products are found at local stores and are commonly kept within households. Those teens experimenting with OTC drugs, prescription drugs, or other substances may go on to develop substance use disorders.

## What You Can Do

As discussed before, communication is key. Start talking to your kids at an early age and do it in an *age appropriate* manner for complete understanding. Start with tobacco use, since people smoke openly in our society. Make it clear to your children that you do not want them using any type of drugs. Don't use scare tactics, but explain the effects, such as: impaired motor skills, memory and concentration; major health conditions; and poor school performance. Also explain that if they use drugs, the people who care about them will be very disappointed.

You will also want to get to know your teen's friends. Invite them over and encourage open discussions about what's happening at school. If you think one of your teen's friends might be using drugs, encourage your teen to distance herself from the friend. It won't be easy, but you have the best interest of your teen in mind. Get her involved in adult-supervised afterschool activities to keep her busy.

Make sure your teen is prepared when faced with the temptation of drugs or alcohol. Let him know you are available to pick him up at a moment's notice, to remove him from a situation, with no questions asked and no consequences. Know where your kids are and have them check in with you.

If you suspect your child uses drugs, get help. Do not shame them. Let him know you are there for him no matter what. Be calm and let him know everything will be OK. Take your child to your family physician. Doctors can help assess whether a teen has a substance use disorder and help to implement the appropriate intervention. Health professionals can perform drug tests and refer you to the appropriate facility for further treatment. Teens should receive services from programs and therapists with expertise in treating adolescents. Teens should not receive the same treatment as adults. Teen programs must be adapted for their particular issues.

# 12

# Sexual Attraction and Orientation

As people pass from childhood through teenhood and into adulthood, it is a natural part of life to have growing sexual feelings. The hormonal and physical changes of puberty during the teen years awaken sexual feelings in new ways. These changes involve both the body and the mind, and teens may wonder about new sexual feelings.

It takes time for people to understand who they are and who to become. Part of the understanding includes a person's sexual feelings and attractions.

## Sexual Orientation

The term sexual orientation refers to the gender—male or female—to which a person is attracted. There are several types of sexual orientations:

- Heterosexual: People who are heterosexual are romantically and physically attracted to members of the opposite sex. Males are attracted to females, and females are attracted to males. Heterosexuals are referred to as straight.
- Homosexual: People who are homosexual are romantically and physically attracted to people of the same sex. Females who are attracted to other females are lesbian; males who are attracted to other males are gay.
- Bisexual: People who are bisexual are romantically and physically attracted to members of both sexes.
- Pansexual (sometimes called omnisexual): People who feel attracted to other people regardless of their gender identities,

61

sex, or sexual orientation. They are attracted to them for *who* they are and not *what* they are.

- Polysexual: People who are attracted to multiple genders and/ or sexes. It should not be confused with polyamory, which is the desire to be intimately involved with more than one person at a time, or pansexuality, which is an attraction to all genders and sexes.
- Asexual: Sometimes referred to as having no sexuality, in its broadest sense, the term means the lack of sexual attraction to others, or the lack of interest in sex. It may also be considered a lack of a sexual orientation.
- Transgender: Transgender is the state of one's gender identity— self-identification as woman, man, neither or both—not matching one's assigned sex or identification by others as male, female, or intersex, based on physical/genetic sex. Transgender does not suggest a specific form of sexual orientation; transgender people may identify as heterosexual, homosexual, bisexual, pansexual, polysexual, or asexual. Some may consider conventional sexual orientation labels inadequate or inapplicable to them.

Teens, both boys and girls, often find themselves having sexual thoughts and attractions. At times these feelings can be so intense that they can be confusing or disturbing. This can be especially true for people who have thoughts about someone of the same sex and automatically think, "Am I gay?"

Thinking sexually about both the same sex and the opposite sex is common as teens sort through their growing sexual feelings. Imagining doesn't necessarily mean a person fits into a particular type of sexual orientation.

There's no right or wrong when your son or daughter tries to explore his or her sexuality. Teens may experiment with sexual experiences, including those with members of the same sex. These experiences, by themselves, do not necessarily mean a person is gay or straight.

## Choice of Sexual Orientation

Most medical professionals believe sexual orientation involves a complex mixture of biology, psychology, and environmental factors. A person's genes and inborn hormonal factors may play a role as well. These medical professionals believe sexual orientation, whatever its causes, is not chosen.

Not everyone agrees. A number of people believe individuals can choose whom they are attracted to, and people who are gay have chosen to be attracted to people of the same gender. No matter what someone's sexual orientation is, in some cases, it may be affected by the life experiences a person has had.

People of different sexual orientations come from all walks of life—rich or poor, educated or non-educated—and can come from all backgrounds and ethnic groups. There are lots of opinions and stereotypes about sexual orientation, and these can be hurtful to people of all orientations. If a person has a feminine look as a male or a masculine look as a female, that doesn't mean the person is homosexual. As with most things, making assumptions based on looks can lead to the wrong conclusions.

## Gay Teens

Disclosing sexual orientation or *coming out* to their parents can be difficult for most teens. For people who are gay or lesbian, it can feel like everyone is expected to be straight. Therefore, gay and lesbian teens may pretend to feel things they don't in order to fit in with others. These teens might feel the need to deny who they are or hide an important part of themselves.

Some gay or lesbian teens tell a few accepting, supportive friends and family members about their sexual orientation. Most teens coming out to their friends and family are fully accepted by them and their communities. These teens feel comfortable about being attracted to someone of the same gender and don't feel confused about it.

Not everyone has the same feelings or an adequate support system. Those who feel the need to hide who they are, or who fear rejection, discrimination, or violence, can be at greater risk for emotional problems like anxiety or depression. They are also more likely to drop out of school, live on the streets, use drugs, alcohol, and even attempt to harm themselves. Fortunately, the majority avoid these hardships.

It can be frustrating for a teen if he or she has the courage to come out, and then the parents tell him or her, "You don't know what you're talking about." Parents may be in denial and truly believe their teen is too young to know his or her sexual orientation, or maybe they simply don't want to believe *they* could have a gay child. Some parents feel that if they act like it isn't possible, then it won't be possible.

Most teens accept the fact of being gay, even if their parents don't understand. If you do not accept your gay teen, he may come out to another adult he can trust, and whom he thinks his parents respect, and ask them to talk to you. Would you want your teenager to have to turn to someone else? It's OK to ask your teen to attend counseling with you so you both can understand and work through the feelings. You have to make it clear up front that you aren't suggesting counseling to try to make him or her straight. The counseling serves as an outlet for everyone to share their feelings and work through them together.

## Talk About It

For teens, talking about sex and sexuality can be embarrassing. The key is to find someone comfortable and knowledgeable who will listen. Teens will look for someone who respects them and whom they can open up to. Wouldn't it be awesome if that person was you?

Places teens can find someone to talk to:

- Home or other close relatives
- School: school counselors/teachers

- Doctor's Office: primary care physician or psychologist/psychiatrists or other trained counselors
- Another teen
- Teen organizations: youth groups composed of teens facing similar issues

Counseling offers a nonjudgmental, caring, and trained therapist who can provide support as you both go through the process of self-exploration and coming out. Although most counselors are sensitive and supportive of gay/lesbian/bisexual orientations, it is important to select a counselor you feel comfortable with. Asking the counselor direct questions about his or her feelings or knowledge about gay/lesbian/bisexual issues can help you determine the right fit. If you are still unsure about the right counselor, ask others for referrals.

Although sexual feelings and behavior are important parts of human development, there are still unanswered questions about human sexuality. Researchers learn new information every day, and people will know more about sexual orientation in the coming years. Whether gay, straight, bisexual, or not sure, all teens have questions about physically maturing and sexual health. This is part of their growth and development. It doesn't have to be difficult. It's part of them finding themselves and growing up to adulthood. Be by their side to give them the support they deserve.

# 13

# Talking About Sex

Sex is not an easy topic of conversation. Most teens think talking to their parents about sex is *gross*! Some parents don't feel the need to have this talk because they think their teen won't have sex until marriage. The talk must happen and sooner than later. If you are unsure how to have the talk with your teen, speak to a professional. Do not depend on your local school system, their peers, teen pregnancy TV shows, or the Internet to teach your kids about sex.

## Communicate

As parents, we can make a difference when we talk with our kids. In fact, teens often name their parents as the biggest influence in their decisions about sex. Teens who report having conversations with their parents about sex are more likely to delay sexual activity, have fewer partners, and use condoms and other contraceptives when they do have sex.

If you have not started talking to your children already, now is the time to start. It is never too late. We all remember our *first time* and what it was like, and no matter what, we want more for our children. It is common for parents to want their children to wait for marriage. But times have changed, and teens aren't waiting to have sex.

It is important to teach our teens about love. When you love someone, sex can be wonderful. Knowing someone for a week, a month, or two months isn't enough. You have to know your partner and his or her history before consenting to having sex.

It is important to ask your teen:

- What is her definition of love?
- What is her idea of affection, both physical and emotional?
- What does she already know about sex?
- How does she feel about relationships in general?
- Who are her role models? Why?

Besides the physical considerations, there are also emotional considerations. Your teen could feel regret, shame, anger, or guilt after a sexual encounter.

You need to ask:

- Have you thought about waiting to have sex until you're an adult?
- Do you know if any of your friends have had sex? Don't ask for names. This will give you a general idea if they talk about it.
- Do you know about contraception, and are you prepared to use it?
- How will you get contraception?
- What if you had sex when you felt you weren't ready, but the other person pressured you, and it turned out to be an unhappy experience?
- What if you become pregnant? What will you do?
- Do you know what human immunodeficiency virus (HIV) is? What if you contracted HIV and developed acquired immune deficiency syndrome (AIDS)? Are you ready to deal with a heavy-duty sickness that could possibly end your life?
- Do you know what a sexually transmitted disease (STD) is?
- What would you do if you contracted an STD?
- What if you passed it on to another person? How would you feel?
- Would you say no if you felt the time and place weren't right?

Again, it is not an easy discussion to have, and you don't have to talk about it all at once. Make it a part of your everyday life when those teachable moments arise. A local news program can lead to discussions about sex. For example, the announcer states: "Coming next: pregnant teen abandons baby," and you have an excellent starter!

## Sexually Transmitted Diseases (STDs)

Sexually transmitted diseases (STDs) are infections passed through sexual contact. There are different infections that can be passed, and their treatments, symptoms, and severity depend on which one is contracted. With the increased numbers of teens having sex, the CDC (Centers for Disease Control) states more than half will contract an STD before the age of twenty-five.

Your teen must know how these infections are contracted and know the signs and symptoms. Impress on your teen that the surest way to avoid STDs is to avoid sexual intercourse. If you think, or know, your teen is having sex, make sure he understands that using any birth control aside from condoms will not prevent an STD. Protection must be used each and every single time they have sex.

The basics on STDs:

- STDs can affect anyone. There is no discrimination involved with STDs. Women and men of all ages, races, and ethnic backgrounds can get STDs.
- You can get an STD by having any variation of sexual contact, including vaginal, anal, and oral sex.
- Several types of STDs can be transmitted through skin-to-skin contact or kissing. This is why it is important your teen knows his or her partner before being intimate.
- Although some STDs can be treated and will go away, others cannot be cured. In cases where there is no cure, you can try to suppress the symptoms and manage the condition.
- If an STD is left untreated, it can lead to serious health complications, including pelvic inflammatory disease, organ damage, infertility, cervical cancer, or even death.

- At times it is often impossible to tell if someone has an STD. Sometimes STDs cause symptoms people can see or feel. But sometimes not. Even if you can't see signs of infection, STDs can still be passed to another person. Also, people confuse symptoms related to certain STDs with something more harmless like a common yeast infection, which is not an STD.

Ways to reduce the risks:

- The most foolproof way to avoid STDs is abstinence.
- Have your teen talk with his or her partner about STDs, sexual history, and how to avoid risks *before* having sex. Open communication encourages trust and respect among partners and helps reduce the risk for STDs.
- Have safe sex. Condoms, both the male and female variety, have a 99 percent effectiveness rate when used consistently and correctly at stopping the spread of most STDs. Condoms made from lambskin, also known as natural condoms, *do not* protect against STDs. All teens must carry protection and cannot rely on the other person to be responsible. It is his or her responsibility to be safe.
- Do not give into a partner who wants to have unprotected sex.
- Limit the number of sexual partners.
- Avoid alcohol and drug use. When drinking or high, it is hard to make the right decisions about sex. Most people admit to doing something while drunk or high that they would not have done when sober.

## Common Types of STDs

- Bacterial Vaginosis (BV): BV is one of the most common forms of vaginal infections. Individuals are commonly asymptomatic, or without symptoms. Symptoms in women include: unpleasant vaginal odor; strong, "fishy smell," especially after intercourse; non-viscous, white or gray, vaginal discharge; burning during urination; and itching around the outside of the vagina. BV can be transmitted through vaginal, anal, or oral sex. It can be treated with antibiotics, and both partners must be treated.

- Chlamydia: Chlamydia is the number one STD in the United States. It's a bacterial infection passed during sexual contact and can infect the penis, vagina, cervix, anus, urethra, eye, or throat. Chlamydia can be cured with antibiotics; however, most teens don't know they have it because chlamydia is often asymptomatic. If left untreated, it can cause serious health problems, such as pelvic inflammatory disease, infertility, and, in men, painful swelling of the testicles.

- Crabs: Also referred to as pubic lice, crabs nest in pubic hair, and the main symptoms are itching and burning of the pubic area. No contraception on the market right now will protect you from crabs. You can get them by touching or being close to someone who has them, even if you don't have sex. The lice can jump from one person to another, and you can also get them by sleeping in a bed, wearing clothes, or sitting on a toilet seat infected with crabs. The lice are typically seen attached to hair in the pubic area, but they may appear in other areas of the body where coarse hair is present, such as a beard, chest hair, and armpits. Crabs are completely treatable with medication. You must also wash all items where there was direct contact with the lice.

- Gonorrhea: Gonorrhea is caused by bacteria that grows and multiplies in the warm, moist areas of your body, including the cervix, uterus, fallopian tubes, urethra, anus, mouth, throat, and eyes. Gonorrhea is serious. If not treated, it can lead to infertility, pelvic inflammatory disease, chronic pelvic pain, and ectopic pregnancy. Gonorrhea is treatable with antibiotics. Both partners must be treated.

- Herpes: Herpes is a common infection caused by two types of viruses that can infect your mouth (oral herpes) or genitals (genital herpes). Herpes is easy to catch and can spread through touching, kissing, and/or sex with an infected person. According to the CDC, a person can only get herpes virus 2 (HSV-2) infection during sexual contact with someone who as a genital HSV-2 infection. Transmission can occur from an infected partner who does not have a visible sore and may not know that he or she is infected. Herpes virus 1 (HSV-1) can cause genital herpes, but it more commonly causes infections of the mouth and lips, so-called "fever blisters." HSV-1 infection of the genitals can be caused by oral-genital or genital-genital contact with a person who has HSV-1 infection. There is no cure for herpes, only symptom management. The most common symptom of genital herpes is a cluster of blistery sores in the genital area. Some people have herpes and are symptom free.

- HIV/AIDS: HIV is passed to sex partners through blood, semen, seminal fluid or pre-cum, and vaginal fluids. You can get HIV from direct contact, such as having vaginal, anal, or oral sex, or sharing injected drug needles and syringes. Sometimes there are no signs of HIV at first. You might not know for sure you've been infected until you get a blood test. People with HIV may look healthy, but they can still transmit HIV. There is no cure. Treatment of symptoms can help people with HIV/AIDS live for years. Condoms offer protection against HIV, which is most often spread through unprotected sex.

- HPV/Genital warts: Human papilloma virus (HPV) affects millions of teens and is spread by skin-to-skin contact during vaginal, anal, or oral sex. HPV can lead to cervical cancer and other genital cancers as well as genital warts. There is no treatment for HPV infection, and most infections disappear. Medication is directed toward the removal of genital warts or precancerous changes in association with the infection. There is an HPV vaccine, which protects against the types of HPV that cause most cases of cervical cancer and the types that cause most cases of genital warts. The vaccine is most effective if given *before* your teen becomes sexually active.

- Syphilis: Syphilis is a sexually transmitted infection caused by bacteria passed from person to person through direct contact with a sore. Sores occur mainly on the genitals, anus, or in the rectum. Sores can also occur on the lips and in the mouth. Syphilis is especially contagious in the early stages of the disease, when the sores are present. Even though it is curable with antibiotics, if syphilis isn't treated, it can cause serious damage to the brain, nerves, eyes, heart, blood vessels, liver, bones, and joints and can eventually lead to death.

Although there are other types of STDs, these are the most common. Teach your teen that with the proper use of condoms and good hygiene most infections can be prevented. Of course, abstinence, or no sex, is best. Our teens will experiment, so prepare them. Wouldn't you rather your teen know what he or she is facing, instead of him or her learning the hard way and possibly ruining his or her life?

Bottom line: Abstinence is best!

# 14

# Birth Control Methods

While talking about sex and STDs, it is important to discuss the various types of birth control methods available. There are at least three types of methods: the most effective methods, methods requiring a doctor's visit, and other methods requiring no doctor's visit.

It's important for a female to visit with a gynecologist *before* having sex in order to establish a general baseline of their reproductive health. This is not always possible, since our teens will experiment without our knowledge. Once you find out your daughter has had sex, make the appointment if you haven't already.

When we refer to effectiveness, we talk about the typical-use numbers gathered from couples of all ages. Typical use means couples who used that particular method of birth control; it accounts for human errors and occasional contraceptive failure. But generally, teens are not as careful as adults in using these methods, so there are no real use rates for teens.

Effectiveness will vary according to use. If you follow the instructions and utilize the contraception as directed, the percentages noted below will apply, which is considered typical use. Please talk to your physician about what type of birth control method will work best for your daughter. Make sure you and your daughter understand all of the potential side effects. Some of the side effects are short lasting, some long lasting, and some can be life threatening.

## 100 Percent Effective

- Abstinence, no sex: The 100 percent method for avoiding pregnancy. This method is best for teens. It eliminates the worry about unplanned pregnancy and STDs as well as all the emotional consequences that come from having sex.

## 90 Percent and Above Effective: Requires a Physician's Visit

- Implanon: This method is effective over 99 percent of the time with typical use. Implanon is a hormone-releasing birth control implant for use by women to prevent pregnancy for up to three years. The implant is a flexible plastic rod about the size of a matchstick containing a progestin hormone called etonogestrel. The healthcare provider will insert the implant beneath the skin of the inner side of the upper arm. Implanon does not protect against STDs.
- IUD (intrauterine device): This method is effective over 99 percent of the time with typical use. An IUD is a small, flexible plastic T-shaped device that the physician inserts into the uterus to prevent pregnancy. There are two types: one can be left in for up to five years, and the other can be left in for up to ten years. IUDs do not protect against STDs.
- Depo-Provera: This method is effective 99 percent of the time with typical use. The contraceptive shot—also known by the brand name Depo-Provera or Depo—is a hormone injection of progestin that physicians give to a woman every three months. Depo works by preventing ovulation, and most women stop having their period after a few months, but it returns when the woman stops using Depo. A health care provider must administer the shot. It requires visits to a clinic or office every three months for a new injection. Missing a shot, or delaying your shot schedule, will lessen the effectiveness of Depo-Provera. Make sure to get the shot on time. Depo will not protect against STDs.

- Birth Control Pills: This method is effective 96-99 percent of the time with typical use. Birth control pills, sometimes called oral contraception, also known as "the pill," are pills females take to prevent pregnancy. Oral contraception works by releasing hormones, either a combination of estrogen and progestin or progestin alone, to prevent ovulation and increase cervical mucus, which blocks sperm. The pill should be taken at the same time every day, and menstruation will occur at the end of each month before the woman starts the next pack of pills. Versions of the pill are available and all differ: different levels of hormones and different types of side effects. If there are side effects from one type, don't give up on the pill altogether; talk to a health care professional to figure out another type of pill to try. Birth control pills are available with a prescription obtained from your health care provider or a family planning clinic. The pill does not protect against STDs.
- Ortho Evra: This method is effective 99 percent of the time with typical use. The Ortho Evra patch is a thin square of plastic—similar to a nicotine patch—that has been treated with hormones. It's sticky on the back, and a woman places it on her skin where it releases the hormones, which her body then absorbs. It can be worn anywhere: a woman's derriere, belly, arm, or upper torso, and each patch is worn for a week and then peeled off and replaced. No patch is worn the fourth week, and menstruation will occur. After the fourth week, the cycle of the patch begins again. A prescription is required, but the woman applies and removes the patch. Ortho Evra does not protect against STDs.
- NuvaRing: This method is effective 99 percent of the time with typical use. The NuvaRing is a thin, flexible ring about two inches across that contains the same hormones as birth control pills and works the same way. The woman inserts the ring into her vagina, where it is held in place by the vaginal walls, and neither she nor her partner can feel it. It stays in for three weeks, slowly releasing hormones, and then the woman removes it the fourth week, when menstruation occurs. After the fourth

week, the woman inserts a new ring. A prescription is required to get the ring, but the woman inserts and removes it herself. NuvaRing does not protect against STDs.

- Diaphragm: This method is effective 80-94 percent of the time with typical use. The diaphragm is a shallow, flexible, dome-shaped cup made of latex. Before sex, the woman inserts it into the vagina; it basically covers the cervix, which makes it tough for sperm to reach an egg. The diaphragm is most effective when it's combined with a spermicide. Diaphragms are tricky because they have to be fitted to the body; therefore, a doctor visit is required. Once obtained, the diaphragm can be used for up to ten years. The diaphragm does not protect against STDs.

## 70–89 Percent Effective: No Physician's Visit

- Sponge: This method is effective 89-91 percent of the time with typical use. The sponge is a round, foam circle about two inches in diameter that is inserted into the vagina before having sex. It blocks the cervix so that sperm can't get through, and it kills sperm by releasing spermicide. Each sponge is made for one-time use and one-size-fits all. You do not need a prescription for the sponge. Sponges are available at drugstores or online. The sponge does not protect against STDs.
- Condoms: This method is effective 85 percent of the time with typical use for male condoms and 75 percent of the time with typical use for female condoms. Condoms, for males, are thin latex or plastic sheaths rolled down over the penis that protect against pregnancy *and* STDs. Female condoms, which are newer, look like bigger male condoms turned inside out. The condom is inserted into the vagina, lining the inside so that no sperm can reach the point where an egg could be fertilized. Condoms should be put on before genital contact and not taken off until after sex is over. The male and female condoms should *not* be used at the same time, but because these are the only birth control methods to protect against STDs, condoms are best used with other types of birth control like the pill or

patch. Contraceptive foam can offer added protection against pregnancy in case a condom breaks. Keep in mind that condoms have an expiration date because the latex can weaken over time. Instruct teens not to store them in a wallet, glove compartment, or places where temperatures can break down the latex, making them less effective. Also, never use condoms with lubricants, like petroleum jelly, because those can reduce their effectiveness, too. Condoms can be purchased at most drugstores and online, or can be picked up at a health clinic or family planning center without a prescription. Female condoms are sometimes harder to find, but they can be purchased online if not found in stores. Female condoms protect against most sexually transmitted diseases, including HIV.

## Emergency Contraception (EC)

The morning-after pill is a type of emergency birth control or contraception. The purpose of emergency contraception is to prevent pregnancy after a woman has had unprotected sex. Morning-after pills contain either levonorgestrel (Plan B One-Step, Next Choice) or ulipristal (ella). These medications are not intended to be used as regular birth control because they are not nearly as effective as other methods in preventing pregnancy, and they have high levels of hormones not meant to be taken over and over again. No EC methods protect you from STDs.

- Plan B One-Step, Next Choice, and ella are the morning-after pills the Food and Drug Administration have approved in the US. Other brands of morning-after pills are available around the world. If age seventeen or older, Plan B One-Step and Next Choice are available over-the-counter—without a prescription—at most pharmacies. If age sixteen or younger, or the teen wants to use ella, a prescription is required from a doctor or health care provider.

No matter what birth control method your teen selects, always reinforce the importance of regular use as directed. As parents, we can provide all of the information needed and hope our sons and daughters will use at least half of it.

Again – Abstinence is best!

# 15

# Pregnancy

The good news: teen pregnancy is on a decline. The bad news: teens still get pregnant. Most teenagers don't plan on getting pregnant, but some do. If you have open communication with your child starting at an early age, and you encourage them to talk to you about *everything*, the chances of your teen getting pregnant lessen significantly. If your daughter gets pregnant, I want to assure you that once you get over the initial shock, it is not the end of the world.

It's unfortunate that television and movies portray being a single teenage mother as acceptable. Yes, some television shows portray some of the struggles teen mothers and fathers face, but does it mean anything to our teens? Our kids see and read about teens with a celebrity status, and they may not fully understand the struggles of being a young mother or father. It is our job as parents to point out what our teens will miss out on now, and later in life, by becoming a teen mom or dad. It is also our responsibility to inform our kids that we don't plan to raise their children. It is our parental instinct to take over and raise our grandchildren, but it is not our responsibility.

## Discussion and Exercise

Include these items in your pregnancy talk:

- Middle school and/or high school: Will she continue to attend the school she is enrolled in, or will she have to transfer to a school that assists unwed teenage mothers?

- Sports: What will happen to his future career in sports? What if he is eligible for a sports scholarship? Would he be able to accept the scholarship, or would he have to turn it down?
- School dances or school trips: Who will watch the child?
- Graduation: Will he graduate with his friends or go for his General Education Development (GED) certificate? What about all of the graduation parties?
- College: Does she want to attend college? Who would take care of the baby?
- Working: Who will watch the child? What type of job will be needed in order to afford a child?
- Food, diapers, clothing, rent, electricity, water, and phone are just some of the expenses. How will he provide for his child? If your teen lives with you, what expenses will be his responsibility?
- Curfews: If your teen lives with you, what curfew will you enforce? Will your teen be allowed to go out with friends on specific nights only?
- Medical: How will she pay the medical bills? What about medical insurance?
- Dating: If the parents aren't married, will they have shared custody of the child? Who will watch the child when he or she goes on dates?

Below is an exercise every parent should go through with his or her teen. Visit in person or go online to a retail department store and write down the cost of the following items. Make two columns. In column one, determine what the cost per item is for one week. In column two, calculate these mostly one-time expenses.

Put these items in column one:

- Diapering: cloth or disposable diapers, wipes or washcloths, powder, diaper ointment, and trashcan liners
- Feeding: formula, baby food, and baby vitamins
- Bath: soaps and lotions
- Laundry: baby laundry detergent

- For mom: nursing bras, breast pads, breast shields, cream for nipples, and panty liners/pads

Put these items in column two:

- Furniture: crib, crib mattress, playpen/play yard, changing table, dresser, sealable trash can, and rocker
- Clothing: one-piece outfits, one-piece pajamas, socks and booties, fleece outfits/sweaters or jacket for winter, mittens, bonnet or cap for summer, and shoes
- Baby gear: car seat (follow the guidelines from the National Highway Traffic Safety Administration on when to use car seats versus booster seats), stroller, highchair, and gym or play arches
- Feeding: bibs, bottles and nipples, and rubber-tipped baby spoons
- Sleep: waterproof crib/mattress liner, fitted sheets, a bumper, and receiving blankets
- Bathing: baby tub, tub seat, slip-resistant bath tub mats, a tub spout cover, washcloths, and hooded towels
- Safety: baby monitor, smoke alarm/carbon monoxide detector, digital thermometer, first aid kit, safety gates, outlet covers, toilet seat latches, and bumpers for sharp-cornered objects
- Miscellaneous: small lamp or nightlight for baby's room, classical or lullaby music, reference books, books you can read to your baby, baby nail clippers, nasal aspirator, stroller toys, and crib toys

Now total up column one and column two. Calculate minimum wage times forty hours. Deduct 20 percent for taxes and another 60 percent for rent, phone, water, electric, and garbage costs. Finally, deduct column one from what is left of the paycheck. Look at the total and ask your teen how they would be able to afford being a new mom or dad. Column two is considered a large one-time expense. Where would that money come from? Teens don't think about the consequences of their actions. Seeing it in *their* handwriting can make a difference.

## Why Teens Become Pregnant

There are reasons why teens become pregnant. Lack of sex education and knowledge of consequences seem to be the two most common reasons. Here are other reasons:

- Rape, sexual abuse, or unwanted sex
- Inconsistent birth control use or unprotected sex
- Lack of instruction on abstinence
- An effort to make a relationship stronger. They want to solidify the relationship and feel connected to the person for the rest of their lives—or so they think.
- For the unconditional love guaranteed from a newborn
- The pregnancy pact. A disturbing trend stemming from peer pressure and the desire to belong to a group.
- Perceived readiness for an adult lifestyle

## High-Risk Groups

Certain girls fall into high-risk categories for teen pregnancy. Teenage girls who may be more likely to become pregnant may also:

- have a mother who was a pregnant teen;
- have siblings who had babies as teenagers;
- have failed academically;
- have lived, or still lives in poverty;
- lack role models;
- be surrounded by drug or alcohol abuse.

When teens have nothing to strive for, becoming parents may seem like their most promising future. Teens fail to see the dangers and complications of having a baby young in life. The responsibility is overwhelming for adults and teens due to simply being unaware of the challenges new parents face. We must make them aware, open their eyes, and encourage them to talk to us about everything. It may be uncomfortable at first, but it's definitely worth it in the long run.

One more time – Abstinence is best!!!

# 16

# Runaway Teens

N o teen is immune to the pressures of growing up or dealing with issues at home. Some teens may become too overwhelmed with problems and may feel like running away is their only way to escape. Many run away because they're afraid of punishments, or they think their home has too many rules and limits. However, other teens run because of a serious issue in their lives. If you fear your child is at risk of running away, open the lines of communication. Teen help starts with communication.

According to the National Center for Missing and Exploited Children, teens cite feeling their parents don't love them or their parents are too strict as the two most common reasons why they run away. And according to the National Runaway Switchboard, an organization that takes calls and helps kids who have run away or those thinking of running away, "Every day between 1.3 and 2.8 million runaway and homeless youth live on the streets of America. One out of every seven children will run away from home before the age of eighteen."

Though most teen runaways return after forty-eight hours to two weeks and move from one friend's house to another, others remain on the streets and never return home. Some teens go to a friend's house or to a relative they can trust and make up stories about their home life. This is a common practice with teens. A parent may suffer pain and humiliation, which is compounded by the need to get their teen help.

Other teenagers who feel they must run farther from home may end up in shelters or, in the worst possible scenario, living on the street. Preferably, a troubled teen will end up at a shelter, as they help provide food and clothing. Some shelters also provide counseling, and some help teens find better living arrangements. Teens who end up homeless on the street may band together with others in their same situation to help each other survive.

## Why Do Teens Run Away?

Here are reasons your teen might feel the need to run away:

- Significant lack of family communication
- Feelings of not belonging or not being good enough
- School problems (for example, bullying)
- Moving to a new area or school
- Substance abuse, either themselves or other relatives at home
- Loss of a parent due to separation, divorce or death
- Problems with parents or blended families (step-parents, step- or half-brothers or sisters)
- Problems with non-parental living situation (other relatives, foster care, or group homes)
- Parental financial difficulty
- Pregnancy
- Abuse, including physical, verbal, sexual, or mental abuse
- Mental health issues
- Need to seek attention
- Questions about sexual orientation
- Following a friend who has run away
- Power of gangs

## Warning Signs of a Troubled Teen

- Poor self-esteem
- Extreme mood changes or rebelliousness
- Isolation or depression
- Suicide threats
- Drop in grades or frequently skipping school
- Withdrawal from family and long-term friends

- New friend's parents don't approve of him or her
- Lying or stealing
- Violent outbursts
- Gang tattoos or paraphernalia
- Possession of a weapon
- Beginning or increased use of drugs or alcohol

## How Do They Survive?

Survival while running away depends on where they end up living. If teens run away to friends, relatives, or shelters, their basic needs are met. Teens who end up on the streets must learn to become independent quickly. The independence may come at a price, since this type of survival is hard.

Methods for survival may include:

- Stealing
- Begging
- Selling drugs
- Prostitution
- Dumpster diving

## What Parents Need to Know

Realizing your child has run away from home is filled with strong emotions, such as anger, fear, and shame that others might think you are not a "good" parent. While some children run across state lines, most children stay close to home. Wherever your teen has gone, there are certain steps necessary not only to ensure a safe return but also to protect both your rights and theirs.

- Try to stay calm. Remember, most runaways return of their own accord.
- Did your teen leave a note? What did he or she pack/take?

- Find out everything you can about the situation. Was it planned or impulsive? Did he or she go off with friends?
- The fact you're looking for your teen is reassurance that you care.
- Have an "open door" attitude to your teen's return.

## What to Do if Your Teen Runs Away

- **Immediately call your local law enforcement agency.**
- When you call law enforcement, provide your child's name, date of birth, height, weight, and any other unique identifiers, such as eyeglasses or braces. Tell them when you noticed your child missing and what clothing he or she was wearing.
- Request that the officer immediately enter your child's name and identifying information into the National Crime Information Center (NCIC) Missing Person File. There's no waiting period for entry into NCIC for children under age eighteen. Get the name and badge number of the officer you speak with. Call back often.
- After you have reported your child missing to law enforcement, call the National Center for Missing & Exploited Children (NCMEC). The toll-free telephone number is: 1-800-THE-LOST (1-800-843-5678).
- Call a national hotline, such as the National Runaway Switchboard (1-800-Runaway).
- Notify relatives and friends.
- Check your teen's items for any clues to their whereabouts. You may also want to check your phone bill for any calls they may have made recently.
- Call the people your teen knows and enlist their help. Search everywhere, but do not leave your phone unattended.

## When Your Teen Comes Home

- Be happy they returned.
- Allow time to settle. Do not start talking about it right away. Your emotions are too high to get anywhere in a conversation. Go two separate directions until you both have gotten some rest.
- Ask and listen. Why did they leave? You may want to evaluate a rule or two after speaking with them, but do not do so while having this talk. Tell them you're willing to think about it, and you will let them know your decision.
- Talk with your teen. Tell them how you felt about them going; let them know they hurt you by leaving. Let them know there isn't a problem you can't solve together. If they ever feel running away might solve something, ask them to talk to you first. You could always offer other choices, so they can make better decisions.
- Get medical attention. If this isn't the first time, or you have problems communicating with your teen when he or she returns, it's time to ask for help. The assistance could be a person your child respects, such as an aunt or uncle, or you may need to seek professional help.

## Prevention

First and foremost, the most important and effective way to stop your teen from running away is to maintain an open and stable relationship with your teen. If you notice any problems they might be having, talk to them before the situation gets out of control. Other tips to improve your relationship with your teen:

- Pay attention. Don't pretend to listen to them.
- Give respect. Acknowledge and support your child's struggle to grow to maturity.
- Don't label. Useless labels will only confuse the real issues you wish to address.

- Create responsibility. Give your teen choices, not orders. Help her understand the consequences of her actions. When punishment needs to be administered, ask what they think would be appropriate. Make sure the punishment fits the "crime" and is consistent with other actions you've taken.
- Administer positive praise. Try to praise your teen instead of criticizing him or her.
- Stop hassling. Asking questions often shuts off information. Let him or her volunteer information.
- Don't always give the answers. Encourage independence and discuss open options to help them develop their problem-solving skills.
- Use teamwork. Work together whenever possible. Identify the problem and find mutually agreeable solutions.

Effective communication is essential. If you are a parent or caregiver in need of assistance, there are local and national programs available. These programs are intended to build life skills, increase knowledge about runaway resources and prevention, educate parents and teens about alternatives to running away, and encourage youth to access and seek help from trusted community members. See the Resources section for more information.

# 17

# Guns, Knives and Other Weapons

On average, 1,300 children die and nearly 5,800 are treated for gunshot wounds each year, according to a July 2017 study from the Centers for Disease Control and Prevention (CDC). That said, I could continue to offer more statistics but let's face it – one death is one too many.

Illegal guns are a source of concern among today's teenagers and parents. Fatal incidents involving teens with guns are making headlines more than ever before. The crimes usually end up with another teen getting shot. Unless you live in a rural area where young adults commonly use guns to hunt, it's possible that a teen carrying a gun has emotional or mental issues and will not hesitate to shoot anyone who gets in his or her way.

## Why Choose a Gun?

Teens choose guns over other weapons because it opens the target area. If a teen targets only one other teen, they may choose to use a knife or other weapon. But, many teens choose weapons that will take care of their "issue" quick and easy.

Teens may compensate for his or her insecurity by "acting big." Having a gun makes them feel powerful. Most like to play the victim, and when they feel like they are the victim, they feel entitled to act out or seek revenge on someone else.

In contrast, teens with good character can act impulsively after they experience a setback (e.g. a bad grade or break-up). These teens may try to reduce the emotional pain through self-harm.

Are our teens cultivating a need for guns based on the messages they see on social media, the TV shows they watch, and/or their music? Many believe so.

## 3 Main Strategies for Reducing Gun Violence:

1.  Reduce children's unsupervised exposure to guns. Research indicates that educational efforts aimed at persuading children and youth to stay away from guns or behave responsibly around them are of limited effectiveness. So, parents must protect children from unsupervised exposure to guns through careful parental monitoring and, if they choose to keep guns in the home, by storing guns locked, unloaded, and separate from ammunition.

2.  Engage communities and strengthen law enforcement. Although research in this area is limited, available evidence suggests that community leaders can promote young people's safety by sending unequivocal messages to youth that gun violence is not an acceptable way to resolve conflict. Law enforcement agencies can partner with community leaders in this effort through community-based policing approaches, which emphasize close collaboration between police and citizens to prevent crime before it occurs.

3.  Limiting the flow of illegal guns to youth. In one national study of male high school sophomores and juniors, 50% of respondents reported that obtaining a gun would be "little" or "no" trouble—even though federal law bans most minors from possessing weapons. Federal and state laws on gun sales should be tightened so that fewer weapons are accessible to youth.

## Recommendations for Parents

Parents need to:

1. Know how a gun safe is secured because kids and teens are becoming aware of safe combinations and where adults stow keys.
2. Know what type of messages -- and from where -- children are receiving, since these messages (e.g. from TV, social media) may glorify gun use and possession.
3. Develop close relationships with their teens. The kinds of relationships that signify to a child it is safe to confide in his or her parent.
4. Encourage teens to assess and speak their feelings as opposed to acting them out.
5. Continually monitor their teens social media apps and text messages for any type of bullying being done to them or by them.

The physical, economic, and emotional toll of gun violence against children and youth is unacceptable. Regardless of one's position regarding adult ownership and use of guns, aggressive efforts are needed by the federal and state governments, working in partnership with local communities and parents, to reduce youth gun violence in the United States.

# 18

# Suicide

S uicide among young people continues to be a serious problem. Suicide is the third leading cause of death for fifteen to twenty-four year olds.

## Reasons

While the reasons teens commit suicide will vary, there are common situations that may lead to these extreme measures. These include:

- Major disappointment
- Stress
- Rejection
- Failure
- Self-doubt
- Pressure to succeed
- Financial uncertainty
- Loss, such as breaking up with a girlfriend or boyfriend
- Failing grades
- Family turmoil, such as divorce or the formation of a new family with step-parents and step-siblings
- A move to a new community

Since the overwhelming majority of those who commit suicide have a mental or substance-related disorder, teens often have difficulty coping with these stressors. Most are unable to see that their lives can turn around and are unable to recognize that suicide is a permanent solution to a temporary problem.

Depression and suicidal feelings are treatable mental disorders. A specialist needs to diagnose the illness and implement appropriate treatment plans for the individual. When parents are in doubt about whether their child has a serious problem, a visit to their family physician or a psychiatric examination can be helpful.

## Signs and Symptoms

Signs and symptoms of suicidal feelings are similar to those of depression. Parents should be aware of the following signs that teens may try to commit suicide:

- Significant loss or gain in appetite
- Withdrawal from friends, family, and regular activities
- Difficulty falling asleep or wanting to sleep all day
- Rebellious behavior, aggressive or destructive actions, or running away
- Neglect of personal appearance
- Extreme personality changes
- Fatigue or loss of energy
- Extreme anxiety or panic
- Feelings of worthlessness or guilt
- Alcohol, drug, or substance use
- Difficulty concentrating or a decline in the quality of schoolwork
- Hallucinations or unusual beliefs
- Frequent complaints about physical symptoms often related to emotions, such as stomachaches, headaches, and fatigue
- Loss of interest in activities they once enjoyed
- No tolerance for praise or rewards
- The suicide of one's parents, or another close family member, could lead to thoughts of such behavior in a teen with a mental or substance-related disorder.

A teenager planning to commit suicide may also:

- give verbal hints with statements such as: "You don't have to worry about me much longer," "Nothing matters," "It's no use," and "I'm a failure;"
- start putting his or her affairs in order, such as giving or throwing away favorite belongings;
- become happy and joyful too quickly after a period of depression;
- have a history of previous attempts to commit suicide.

## What You Can Do

If a child or adolescent says, "I want to kill myself" or "I hope I don't wake up in the morning," always take the statement as serious. People often feel uncomfortable talking about death. One of the most common misconceptions about talking with someone who might be contemplating suicide is that bringing up the subject could make things worse. *Not* true. Bringing up the question of suicide and discussing it without showing shock or disapproval is one of the most helpful things you can do. You show that you take them seriously and that you will respond to his or her need for help.

Never assume someone intending to end his or her life cannot be stopped. If one or more of these signs occur, talk to your son or daughter about your concerns and seek professional help from a physician or a qualified mental health professional. With support from family and the appropriate treatment, suicidal teens can heal and return to a healthier pathway for their life.

Did you know in Florida there is a process called "Baker Act"? It is a lengthy statute, but bottom line: the law says someone can be Baker Acted when "abnormalities of thought, mood, or behavior" are psychiatric in nature. In other words, if someone is freaking out it must be clear it's a psychiatric issue. A trained mental health professional or therapist should know. A parent or cop may not. So, if someone appears to be a threat to him/herself or others, you can take them to the nearest hospital and start the process. Sounds easy – it's not. But, if it will save lives of others, it is worth it.

Check to see what is available in your state. Know the process and follow it. You could save the life of others.

# 19

# Parenting Styles

N ow that you understand the challenges your teens may face, you need to determine your current parenting style, and think about your parents' style, and then determine which one will work best for your family. Take time to reflect on your past and think about what you want for the future. What type of relationship have you had with your child up until now? What type of relationship do you want with your teen?

A parenting style involves a child rearing behavior (of parents, guardians, or other primary caregivers) that involves the amount of control over a child's activities and behavior and the degree of nurturance of the child. Parents can create their own styles from a combination of factors, and these can change over time as the children develop their own personalities and move through life's stages. Is there one style that works best for all teenagers? No. Parenting styles are affected by both the parents' and child's temperaments and is largely based on the influence of one's own parents and culture. Most people learn parenting practices from their own parents. These parents can decide to accept or discard those practices.

## Sample Styles

There are many types of parenting styles, a sample of which is listed below; however, we will discuss the first five categories in more detail:

- Authoritative: These parents are demanding and responsive, as characterized by a child-centered approach, and they hold high expectations of maturity for the child.

- Indulgent or Permissive Parenting: These parents are responsive but not demanding, they are also called lenient and are characterized as having few behavioral expectations for the child.
- Christian Parenting: These parents use the application of Biblical principles on parenting. Some Christian parents follow a strict and more authoritarian interpretation of the Bible, and others are "grace-based" and share other methods.
- Attachment Parenting or Natural Parenting: These parents seek to create a strong emotional bond and avoid physical punishment.
- Helicopter Parenting: Helicopter parents keep their children at close range, always "hovering" above them, trying to make sure no harm will come to them.
- Authoritarian: These parents are demanding but *not* responsive (Strict Parenting), characterized by high expectations on conformity and compliance to parental rules and directions, while allowing little open dialogue between parent and child.
- Positive Parenting: Positive parenting is about empowering children.
- Conscious Parenting or Unconditional Parenting: These parents show love unconditionally rather than conditionally. They are against positive reinforcement parenting, meaning if the child behaves, the parent will show him love, and if he doesn't, the parent will not show him love.
- Slow Parenting: This style encourages parents to plan and organize less for their children, instead allowing them to enjoy their childhood and explore the world at their own pace.
- Negligent or Uninvolved Parenting: Neglectful parenting is neither demanding nor responsive, also called hands-off parenting. The parents are low in responsiveness and do not set limits.
- Nurturant Parenting: A family model where children are expected to explore their surroundings with the protection of their parents.

- Narcissistic Parenting: These parents thirst for external recognition and acceptance and unconsciously use their children as a means to live out dreams and fantasies they never got to realize.
- Toxic Parenting: These parents range from neglecting children's needs to direct physical, emotional, and sometimes even sexual abuse.
- Shared Parenting: This style results when married parents equally share the responsibility of parenting and the responsibility of earning money.
- Punishment-based Parenting: These parents use pain, punishment, intimidation, yelling, degradation, humiliation, shame, guilt, or other things to hurt a child's self-esteem, or they hurt them physically. Punishment-based parenting also damages the relationship between the parent and child. It puts unnecessary pressure on the child, and the child is less apt to perform due to pressure.

## Authoritative

An authoritative parenting style results when there is high parental responsiveness and high parental demands. These parents will set clear standards for their children, monitor the limits set, and also allow children to develop a sense of self. The authoritative parenting style has been most consistent in terms of being associated with positive outcomes for children, such as: a high level of self-esteem, high academic performance, well-developed social skills, and emotional control. Authoritative parents set limits and demand maturity, but when they punish a child, the parents will explain their motives for their punishment. Punishment is measured and consistent, not random or violent.

Typical traits of authoritative parents:

- They are warm and responsive and strive toward meeting their children's physical and emotional needs. They provide rules and guidance without being overbearing.

- They offer relative freedom of choice by encouraging independent thinking and give-and-take discussions.
- They will forgive and teach, instead of punishing the child if he or she falls short.
- They were raised in a spirit of disciplined conformity, general obedience, and adherence to rules. Basically, the children do what they are told to do.
- They produce children who are more independent and self-reliant.

The authoritative parent leads by example, realizing she is a role model to her children. But the authoritative parent also acknowledges that no one is perfect, least of all himself or his children, and apologizes when a situation requires it.

## Indulgent or Permissive Parenting

Indulgent parents, sometimes referred to as permissive parents, make fewer demands of their children. These parents do not discipline their children, because they have relatively low expectations of maturity and self-control. These parents are more responsive than demanding. They are nontraditional and lenient, do not require mature behavior, allow considerable self-regulation, and avoid confrontation. Permissive parents are nurturing and communicative with their children, often taking on the status of a friend more than a parent. Children of permissive parents tend to experiment and be more problematic as teens and young adults.

Typical traits of indulgent parents:

- They meet the child's needs and is warm, responsive, and caring.
- They do not require children to regulate themselves.
- They use a nonrestrictive child-discipline strategy.
- They tend to evade conflicts, embrace harmony, and encourages give-and-take discussions.
- They encourage independent thinking.

Since indulgent parents do not require their children to regulate themselves or behave in an appropriate manner, people feel this can result in the creation of spoiled brats or spoiled sweet children, depending on the behavior of the child.

## Christian Parenting

The basics of biblical parenting involve more than simply raising a child. When we adopt God's standards as our own, we produce a quality character different from a child's natural inclinations. As parents turn to the Bible for instruction, they are able to open up channels in their children's lives for God's grace to flow.

Typical traits of Christian parents:

- They teach their children about formalized religion and religious practices.
- They teach children to memorize and meditate on scripture.
- They nourish their children with wholesome discipline and encourage them to build a personal relationship with God and to live a Christian life.
- They teach their children about forgiveness.
- They adhere to a clean life free of drugs, smoking, and other outside temptations.
- They encourage honesty and truthfulness.

Christian families pray together and stay together. There is often a strong bond between parent and child throughout childhood and into adulthood.

Our society has been moving away from the Church and God. They have removed God from our schools. Christian Parents know how important it is to restore this to all and therefore, make strong believers of their children to carry on to future generations.

## Attachment or Natural Parenting

The aim of attachment parenting is to strengthen the intuitive, emotional, and psychological bond between the primary caregiver, which is usually the mother, and the child. These parents believe that if an infant's emotional and physical needs are quickly and consistently met, the child will build a positive attitude to life, believing he or she is unconditionally loved and that the world is a safe place.

Typical traits of attachment or natural parents:

- They seek to create a special bond.
- They respond with sensitivity.
- They practice positive discipline. Parents are encouraged to work out a solution together with a child, rather than spanking or simply imposing their will on the child.
- They strive for balance in personal and family life. Parents are encouraged to create a support network, live a healthy lifestyle, and prevent parenting burnout.

It's all about going back to the basics. Follow your instincts. You've been a parent for a few years now. You know your child like the back of your hand. Don't complicate things by doing the right and natural thing to show love and compassion to your teenager.

## Helicopter Parenting

Helicopter parents, also called overprotective parents, keep their children at close range, "hovering" above them, trying to make sure no harm will come to them. These overprotective strategies are driven by fears of "losing" control. They react to the fear by taking a protective and aggressive stance toward the world. Helicopter parents are accused of being obsessed with their child's education, safety, extracurricular activities, and other aspects of their child's life.

Typical traits of helicopter parents:

- Helicopter parents don't believe their children can take care of themselves, and they fear that if they don't keep tight control over everything, harm will come to their children.
- They often over-program their children and fail to allow them free time to play and explore on their own.
- They are well known in the school system.
- They will complete basic tasks for their children, such as: homework, job applications, and college applications.
- They will try to solve all of their problems and sweep all obstacles out of the way.

While every parent is convinced her child is "special," is it her distinct responsibility to inform the world, or does some responsibility and advocacy rest in the lap of the child? Should the helicopter land and allow for some self-expression and showmanship originating from the child? Only those parents can answer.

## Outcomes

No one parenting style is right or wrong. Parenting is a lifelong job of trials and errors, and hindsight is always 20/20. All parents must decide for themselves how to raise their children. There are no fixed rules, no written instructions, and no child manual. There are situations in all of our lives that influence the way we do things, both consciously and subconsciously. The way we were raised, and the time and placed we were raised in, are all factors that play an important role in how we raise our children. Parents should keep an open mind to the choices other parents make, learning about the parenting styles of other cultures, and consider if there are things we could all be doing differently. No two kids are alike. What works for one child may not work for another. Find what works for *your* child.

# 20

# Grieving Your Loss

The death of a teenager is a tragedy no matter what happened. Parents feel particularly guilty when it was an accident or suicide. The major cause of death for teenage boys is accidents. They think they are indestructible. Skate boards, bicycles, surfing, rushing everywhere, so full of life. The leading cause of death for teenage girls is suicide.

We point out the dangers, give advice on safety and safety gear, and hope they make the right decisions. They have the pressures of first love and acceptance by the "in" group. Adulthood is looking scary. Peer group pressure is paramount at this stage.

Parents can be aware of trouble and try to reach out to their child. Yet, when the worst happens and a suicide occurs, the guilt can be overwhelming.

Depression is difficult to diagnose. Even Consultant Psychiatrists have a difficult time diagnosing depression. But, most parents have raised their children from the start and know their usual state of being. Even if you were not there from birth, when you spend enough time with a child you get to know their habits. When a child gets out of line, or just starts being "different" parents must take notice and take action.

## Adult Steps of Grieving

The grieving process does not happen in a step by step or orderly fashion. Grieving tends to be unpredictable. Sad thoughts and feelings will come and go like a roller coaster ride. Early on, you may sense a lifting of numbness and sadness and experience a few days without tears. Then, for no apparent reason, the intense grief may strike again.

While grieving may make you want to isolate yourself from others and hold it all in, it's important that you find some way of expressing your grief. Use whatever mode of expression works for you. Many express grief by talking, writing, creating art or music, or being physically active.

Spirituality often is part of the grieving process. You may find yourself looking for or questioning your higher power over a loss. You may gain comfort from your religious or spiritual beliefs. You might also doubt your beliefs in the face of a traumatic or senseless loss. It is so important now to turn to your higher power. When God brings you to it, he will bring you through it. You must keep the faith.

The 5 stages of grief and loss are: Denial and Isolation; Anger; Bargaining; Depression; and Acceptance. People who are grieving do not always go through the stages in the same order or experience all stages.

**Denial & Isolation.** The first reaction to learning about the loss or death of a loved one is to deny the reality of the situation. People often think "this isn't happening" or "this can't be happening." It is a normal reaction to rationalize our overwhelming emotions. Denial is a defense mechanism that buffers the immediate shock of the loss, numbing us to our emotions. We block out the words. We start to believe that life is meaningless, and nothing is of any value any longer. For most people, this stage is a temporary response that carries us through the first wave of pain.

**Anger.** As the masking effects of denial and isolation begin to wear, reality and the pain re-emerge. Most are not ready. The intense emotion is deflected from our vulnerable core, redirected and expressed instead as anger. The anger may be aimed at inanimate objects, complete strangers, friends or family. Anger may be directed at our deceased loved one. Rationally, we know the person is not to be blamed. Emotionally, however, we may resent the person for causing us pain or for leaving us.

Remember, grieving is a personal process that has no time limit, or one "right" way to do it.

**Bargaining**. The normal reaction to feelings of helplessness and vulnerability is often a need to regain control through a series of "If only" statements, such as:

- If only we listened to them…
- If only we had sought medical attention sooner…
- If only we had tried to be a better person toward them…

This is an attempt to bargain. Secretly, we may make a deal with God or our higher power in an attempt to postpone the inevitable, and the accompanying pain. This is a weaker line of defense to protect us from the painful reality. Guilt often accompanies bargaining. We start to believe there was something we could have done differently to have helped save our loved one.

**Depression**. Two types of depression are associated with mourning. The first one is a reaction to practical implications relating to the loss. Sadness and regret predominate this type of depression. We worry about the costs and burial. We worry that, in our grief, we have spent less time with others that depend on us. This phase may be eased by simple clarification and reassurance. We may need helpful cooperation and a few kind words. The second type of depression is different and, in a sense, perhaps more private. It is our quiet preparation to separate and to bid our loved one farewell. Sometimes all we need is a hug.

**Acceptance**. Reaching this stage of grieving is a gift not afforded to everyone. Death may be sudden and unexpected or we may never see beyond our anger or denial. It is not a mark of bravery to resist the inevitable and to deny ourselves the opportunity to make our peace. This phase is marked by withdrawal and calm. This is not a period of happiness and must be distinguished from depression.

Coping with loss is a deep personal and singular experience. No one can help you go through it or understand all the emotions that you're going through. But others can be there for you and help comfort you through this process. The best thing you can do is to allow yourself to feel the grief as it comes over you. Resisting it only will prolong the natural process of healing.

## Teens Steps of Grieving

Teens grieve differently than adults. Their behavior may range from cold and withdrawn to clingy, and they may not always be able to clearly express their needs. Although teens will still experience many of the steps above, they are not fully developed in different areas to handle.

For example:

- Brain
    - o Grey matter (thinking part of the brain) experiences huge growth spurts
    - o Frontal cortex (reasoning, planning, judgment, impulse control) not fully developed until age 23–26
    - o Ability to take in, process, organize and understand information not fully developed
    - o Ability to judge situations, people and behaviors not developed (Teens may experiment with risky behaviors and make poor decisions not considering the consequences.)
    - o Less balanced behavior and decision-making
    - o Rely more on amygdale (portion of the brain that releases gut reactions)

- Body
    - o Physical growth spurts
    - o Puberty—changes in hormones
    - o Sexual development
    - o More sleep needed

Teens will:

- Want and need to be included in important decisions.
- Not want to be treated like a child.
- Need to work through grief in their own way—not your way.
- Need the space and respect that adults get.
- Feel pain just like adults.
- Not want to stand out from other peers.
- Have limited resources available to them.
- Already have a full-time job growing up; grief makes this tough job harder.
- Experience and express grief in an on-again and off-again way for a longer period of time. Sometimes they just have to shelve their grief for another time.

Teens need to understand the following:

- Let your needs be known.
- Don't worry about burdening others.
- Need to speak up to feel better.
- Protecting others from grief is not your responsibility.
- Give others the opportunity to express themselves.
- Be patient and gentle with yourself as you face this new territory.
- Understand and accept that everyone grieves in different ways.
- Be open to communication.
- Ask for help when you need it as your role in the family changes.
- Be open to outside help.
- Find someone at school or work that you trust.
- Maintain your routines with meals, exercise, school and your social life.
- Dose it. Grief can be overwhelming to deal with all at one time, so break it into smaller workable pieces or chunks. It's OK to take a break and do the things you did before. For example, go to the movies with friends.
- Develop a plan for those moments when you are overwhelmed—a safe place to go or a safe person to speak with.

- Write down the changes you are experiencing to help make sense of your thoughts and feelings. Know that it is okay to remember those you love. Even though they are not present in a physical form, they are a part of who you are and will always be with you.

## Moving Forward

Celebrate their life and talk about the memories. There will be tears, but there will be lots of laughter too. You CAN be happy for the life they had. Do not be scared to talk happily about your teenager and celebrate the life he or she had and the friends they shared. If a birthday arrives, don't sit idle. Remember the wonderful years - the holidays, family meals, and parties. Continue to celebrate the love you have for them.

It may be hard to believe in the moment, but everyone keeps going every day despite major losses in life. And you can too. Remember that time helps, but it might not cure. Time has the ability to make that acute, searing pain of loss, less intense. Time makes your emotions less painful, but your feelings of loss and emptiness may never completely go away. Accepting and embracing your new 'normal' might help you reconcile your loss.

There are many support groups you can join. Many people find it helpful to talk with others who have gone through the same type of loss. Don't let others tell you how to feel. Your grief is your own and no one can tell you when it is time to "move on" or "get over it." Allow yourself to feel whatever you want to feel without embarrassment or guilt.

Don't go it alone. Please know that there are others going through something like to you. It is normal to feel as if you are the only person who has suffered such a great loss. Reach out to anyone you feel comfortable with. Don't internalize, your other family members and friends need you. And – most importantly – you need them.

# Conclusion

What a difficult life a teenager leads today. Are our teens forced to live on the edge? Do they experience no acceptance and minimal positive affirmation from parents? Is the peer pressure too much? Are they learning to live from the Internet or TV with no emphasis on moral values or excellence? Are you comfortable with your current parenting style? Or, do you need to tweak some things? Only you can answer these questions.

With all that you have learned in the preceding chapters, I hope you are now fired up to do what you can to protect our kids. There are so many kids out there that need your help and there are parents that have no idea what to do. Step up. Be a volunteer. Reach out to your neighbors and let's all pull together for the sake of our future generations.

As parents, guardians, or caregivers, we should all be taking the following actions:

- Be their parent, their moral compass, their guide, not their friend. Teenagers emulate those they know best.
- Teens hate when their parents fight. Keep your differences behind closed doors.
- Teens need their home to be a refuge, a safe haven.
- Encourage your teen to be an individual, not a follower, and encourage independence.
- Give him or her unconditional love. Your teen really loves you.
- Take responsibility for what you expose your small children and teens to.
- Monitor television, computers, cell phones, and other communication devices. Set and reinforce limits on your teen's media use. Watch TV and movies together to better

connect. Discuss the messages sent about body image and other expectations.

- Provide a healthy and complete meal and sit down together as a family to enjoy it. Use mealtime to talk about things going on in each other's lives.
- Build the lines of communication. Always communicate in a positive manner. Never give them an "I told you so" response. Let them know they can talk to you about *anything*.
- The most important part of communication is being able to hear what isn't being said.
- Respect his or her opinion and take into account his or her thoughts and feelings. It's important your teen knows you are listening.
- Engage in active listening. Active listening is a communication technique that requires the listener to understand, interpret, and evaluate what is heard. Once you hear your teen's concerns, you will be able to feel what he or she feels. Active listening gives the teen the opportunity to correct you. In other words: they talk, you listen, and you paraphrase what they said to you, and the teen tells you if you are correct. Doing so helps to fix any misunderstandings.
- Be honest and direct when talking about sensitive subjects such as sex, drugs, drinking, weapons and smoking.
- Teens want the chance to be trusted. Give them a chance.
- Be willing to admit you don't know everything and that you're not always right.
- Provide a supportive and encouraging environment. Focus on the positive, instead of criticizing. Praise their special talents and nurture their interests. Teens want their parents to be proud of them.
- Model and teach positive stress management and coping skills. Teens need help managing the stresses and pressure in their lives.
- Establish rules, set limits, and ensure conformity to those rules and limits. Post the list of rules where they can see it.
- Know your kid's friends and their parents.

- Never shame them when you find out something you don't approve of. Even "good" kids act out once in a while.
- Help your small children and teens build their self-esteem by teaching them techniques of goal achievement. Have them break down their big goals into small, achievable goals in order to alleviate some of the stress in their lives.
- Look out for signs of stress, anxiety, lack of concentration, poor food and drink intake, personal hygiene changes, sleep disturbances, lack of interest in social activities, and then address them immediately.
- Keep the medicine cabinet locked. Unlocked medicine cabinets are an open invitation for teens and their friends to abuse prescription drugs.
- Keep your gun safes locked and do not give them the combination, or key, under any circumstances.
- If your teen wants to learn about firearms, enroll them to the appropriate course. Supervise them at all times. Do not keep the firearm and the ammo in the same place.
- Know that addiction runs in families and be proactive to prevent it.
- Know that addiction is a health problem and can be treated.
- Understand alcohol, tobacco, and substance abuse is preventable.
- Understand there is **no shame** in accepting professional help.
- Everyone goes through the grieving process differently. Allow others to grieve. Be there for them, even if at a distance. Support is everything.
- Go to church. A family that prays together, stays together. Encourage your teen to join Christian groups. Be a role model and join a Christian parenting group.
- Step up and take action. It's easier to apologize for a misunderstanding, than to apologize to a parent who lost their teen and you could have taken action to help. Teach your children to do the same.

I believe parents do their best with what they know. However, parents are not always aware of the dangers out there. I hope this book has provided you with:

(1) the tools and information you need to be there for your son, daughter, niece, nephew or neighbor;
(2) the ability to understand what issues our teens may face; and
(3) the help and guidance needed to make the appropriate life choices.

We all know teens will still experiment despite our actions to prevent it. We can be comfortable knowing we informed them of the dangers, and we can hope the knowledge of those dangers outweigh their curiosity.

# Resources/Referrals

You can find reliable resources on the Internet and in your city; here are a few of the recognized resources for parents and teens. Feel free to perform an Internet search to find more in your area. Please note: I have no affiliation with these agencies.

Al-Anon Family Groups
Website: http://www.al-anon.alateen.org

America's Pregnancy Helpline
Phone: 1-866-942-6466
Website: http://www.thehelpline.org

American Academy of Child & Adolescent Psychiatry
Website: http://www.aacap.org

American Cancer Society
Website: http://www.cancer.org

American Foundation for Suicide Prevention
Phone: 1-888-333-AFSP (2377) (toll-free)
Website: http://www.afsp.org

Anti-Hate: Not in Our Town
Working together for safe, inclusive communities
Website: http://www.niot.org

Bible Gateway
The Word for all the World
https://www.biblegateway.com/

Cable News Network (CNN)
Website: http://www.cnn.com

Centers for Disease Control and Prevention
Diseases and Conditions/Healthy Living/Injury, Violence & Safety/
Data & Statistics
Website: http://www.cdc.gov

Children Now
Phone: 510-763-2444 x 119
Fax: 510-763-1974
Website: http://www.childrennow.org

Drug Enforcement Administration (DEA)
Website: http://www.dea.gov

Focus Adolescent Services: Runaway and Missing Children
Website: http://www.focusas.com/runaways.html

Free Quit Smoking Tips
Website: http://www.tobaccofree.org

Gay/Lesbian Issues
LYRIC (Lavender Youth Recreation and Information Center)
Website: http://www.lyric.org

PFLAG (Parents, Families and Friends of Lesbians and Gays)
Website: http://www.pflag.org

Journal of Pediatrics
Website: http://www.jpeds.com

Kids Health
Website: http://www.kidshealth.org and http://www.teenshealth.org

National Campaign to Prevent Teen and Unplanned Pregnancy
Website: http://www.thenationalcampaign.org

National Center for Missing and Exploited Children
Phone: 1-800-THE-LOST (1-800-843-5678)
Website: http://www.missingkids.com

National Children's Coalition
Website: http://www.teenzeen.org

National Domestic Violence Hotline
Phone: 1-800-799-SAFE (7233) or TTY 1-800-787-3224
Website: http://www.thehotline.org

National Eating Disorders Association
Website: http://www.nationaleatingdisorders.org

National Highway Traffic Safety Administration
Website: http://www.nhtsa.gov/Safety/CPS

National Runaway Switchboard
Phone: 1-800-RUNAWAY (786-2929)
http://www.1800runaway.org

National Sexual Assault Hotline
RAINN: Rape, Abuse & Incest National Network
Phone: 1-800-656-HOPE (4673)
Website: http://www.rainn.org

National Suicide Prevention Lifeline
Phone: 1-800-273-TALK (8255): Suicide hotline, 24/7 free and
confidential, nationwide network of crisis centers
Website: http://www.suicidepreventionlifeline.org

Pacer's National Bullying Prevention Center
Website: http://www.pacer.org/bullying

Planned Parenthood Federation of America
Phone: 1-800-230-PLAN (7526)
Website: http://www.plannedparenthood.org

S.A.F.E. Alternatives
Self-Abuse Finally Ends
Phone: 1-800-DONTCUT (366-8288)
Website: http://www.selfinjury.com

US National Library of Medicine
Website: http://www.nlm.nih.gov

# Appendix A

## Cell Phone Contract

The contract should include the following:

- I will stick to the usage allowed with our cell phone plan, and I will not go over the limits of usage.
- I know I am required to contribute to the cost of my cell phone (if applicable). My contribution is _____ a month/week.
- My cell phone must be turned off at _____ each night.
- It's my responsibility to recharge the cell phone each night.
- I agree that if I am unable to keep up with my promises, the use of my cell phone will be taken away from me. My phone can be taken away even if I have contributed to the cost of the cell phone plan.
- I will not use my cell phone to take pictures or video of nudity, violence, or other unlawful activities.
- I will not use my cell phone to call anyone for malicious purposes.
- I will not use my cell phone while driving.
- I will limit the number of people who have my cell phone number.
- I will not use my cell phone in class to text my friends.
- I will not answer calls from numbers I do not recognize.
- I will not post my number to social media websites.
- I will not download anything onto my phone without permission.
- I know having the use of a cell phone is a privilege. I agree this privilege creates great responsibility.
- I respect that my parents love me and want to keep me safe.
- I agree to allow my parents to see the stored information on my phone in the event they feel I'm not being honest with them.

_____          _____
Parent Signature                                                    Teen Signature

_____
Date

# Index

# B

Baby Gear, 81
Bacterial Vaginosis (BV), 69
Bargaining 104-5
Begging, 85
Binge Drinking, 56
Binge Eating Disorder, 9, 12-13
Biological Clocks, 19
Bipolar Disorder, 41
Birth Control. See Also Sexual
    Intercourse
    About, 68, 73-78
    Condoms, 28, 66, 68-69, 71-72,
      76-77
    Contraceptive Foam, 77
    Depo-Provera, 74
    Diaphragm, 76
    Implanon, 74
    Intrauterine Device (IUD), 74
    Morning-After Pill, 77
    Nuvaring, 75-76
    Ortho Evra, 75
    Pills, 28, 75, 77
    Spermicide, 76
    Sponge, 76
Bisexual, 61, 62, 65
Blended Families, 84
Blistery Sores, 71
Body Image
Binge Eating Disorder And, 13
    Concerns About, 2
    Media Images Of, 9, 93
    Poor Nutrition and Negative, 7
    Unhealthy, 3
Body Piercings, 25
Bone Breaking, 40
Boredom, 9, 12
Botox, 17
Boundaries, 4, 34
Boys
    Intermittent Explosive Disorder, 43
    Nutrition And, 7
    Physical Changes, 1–3

Puberty, 1
Branding, 40
Breaking Up with Girlfriend or
    Boyfriend, 92
Breast Pads, 81
Breasts, 1
Breast Shields, 81
Bruising, 35. See Also Physical Abuse
Bulimia Nervosa, 9-10
Bullying. *See Also* Cyberbullying
    About, 4, 32, 33, 36, 84, 91
Burning, 40

# C

Caffeine, 20
Calcium, 6-7
Cancers, 7, 55, 68, 71
Car Accidents, 19
CDC. *See* Centers For Disease Control
Cell Phone, 4
Cyberbullying And, 32
    Date Rape And, 50
    Health Risks Of, 52
    Restrictions on Usage, 53
    Sexting, 52-54
    Usage Contract, 54
Centers For Disease Control, 48, 68, 89
Cervical Cancer, 68, 71
Chaperone, 48
Chat Rooms, 31, 36
Chemical Substances, 4
Child Pornography, 52
Child Rearing Behavior, 87. *See Also*
    Parenting Style
Children Now, 114
Chlamydia, 70
Christian Parenting, 97, 100
Cigarettes. See Smoking
Cognitive Behavioural Therapy, 45
Coming Out, 63. See Also Homosexual
Communication,
    About Sex, 69, 79
    Active Listening And, 110

# N

Name-Calling, Virtual, 32. *See Also* Cyberbullying
Naps (Sleep), 20
Narcissistic Parenting, 98
Narcolepsy, 19, 21
Narcotic Pain Drugs, 58
National Campaign to Prevent Teen and Unplanned Pregnancy, 114
National Center For Missing & Exploited Children, 86
National Children's Coalition, 115
National Crime Information Center Missing Person File, 86
National Domestic Violence Hotline, 115
National Eating Disorders Association (NEDA), 115
National Highway Traffic Safety Administration, 115
National Runaway Switchboard, 83, 86, 115
National Sexual Assault Hotline, 115
National Suicide Prevention Lifeline, 115
National Survey on Drug Use and Health (NSDUH), 58
Natural Parenting, 97, 101
NCMEC. See National Center For Missing & Exploited Children
NEDA. *See* National Eating Disorders Association
Negligent or Uninvolved Parenting, 97
Nerds, 24
Nicotine, 20
    Patch, 75
Nightmares, 23
Nipple Cream, 81
Nocturnal Emissions, 2
NSDUH. *See* National Survey on Drug Use and Health
Nursing Bras, 81
Nurturant Parenting, 97

Nutrition
    Anorexia Nervosa And, 10
    Binge Eating Disorder And, 12-13
    Bulimia Nervosa, 11
    Counselling, 10
    Eating Disorders And, 7–8
    Obesity And, 8
    Poor, 6, 8, 57
    Proper, 7
Nuvaring, 75

# O

Obesity, 8-9
Obsessive-Compulsive Disorder, 41
Oily Skin, 16
Omnisexual, 61
Online Passwords, 31
Open Communication, 68, 79
Open-Door Policy, 86
Opposite Sex Interest, 2, 61-62
Oral
    Appliances, 23
    Contraception, 75
    Genital Contact, 71
    Herpes, 65
    Sex, 68, 70 -71 *See Also* Sexual Intercourse
Ortho Evra, 75
Osteoporosis, 6, 10
Other Weapons 89

# P

Pacer's National Bullying Prevention Center, 115
Pansexual, 61-62
Panty Liners/Pads, 81
Parental
    Attitudes and Behavior, 55
    Authoritative 98
    Blocks, 53
    Burnout, 101
    Control 31

# About the Author

MICHELE SFAKIANOS (Sfa-can-iss) is a Registered Nurse, Leading Authority on Parenting and Life Skills, Life Transformation Specialist, Speaker and an award-winning Author. In 1982, she received her *AS Degree in Business Data Processing/Computer Programming*. In 1993, she received her *Associate in Science degree in Nursing* from St. Petersburg Junior College, graduating with Honors. In 1999, Michele received her *Bachelor of Science degree in Nursing* from Florida International University, graduating with High Honors. Michele is the owner of Open Pages Publishing, LLC offering quality self-publishing. Her first book "Useful Information for Everyday Living" was published October 2010 and was later changed to "The 4-1-1 on Life Skills" and released June 2011. Her other books include: "The 4-1-1 on Step Parenting," released October 2011; "The 4-1-1 on Surviving Teenhood," released October 2012; "Parenting with an Edge," released June 2013; and "Teen Success: It's All About You! Your Choices – Your Life," also released June 2013; "Ace Your Life," released June 2014; "Building Leadership through Self-Insight," released October 2015; "Parenting Plan," released November, 2015; and "The 4-1-1 on Reinventing You," released August 4, 2016. She is well respected in her areas of expertise. Her years of experience as a Registered Nurse, Personal Life Transformation Specialist, Mother, and Grandmother, have given her the knowledge and wisdom to write her books.

Michele has won several awards for her writing such as: Indie Excellence Winner Book Awards; Living Now Book Awards; USA Best Book

Award Finalist; Wise Bear Digital Book Awards; Readers Favorite Book Awards; and many more.

Michele is also the owner of Take Action with Michele. She is a John Maxwell Certified Personal Coach, Speaker and Educator. Michele wants to help you reach your full potential and live your best life possible. Visit www.takeactionwithmichele.com for more information.

Michele lives in Estero, Florida, where she works, writes, speaks, and supports individuals and families in living a life of enrichment and empowerment.

**Open Pages Publishing, LLC**

**Open Pages Publishing** is a self-publishing company offering books to inspire, teach, and inform readers. We specialize in a variety of subjects including: life skills, self-help, reference, parenting, leadership and teens.

Ordering Information:

Open Pages Publishing books are available at online bookstores. They may also be purchased for educational, business, or promotional use:

- For bulk orders: special discounts are available on bulk orders. For details contact our sales staff at info@openpagespublishing.com.

If you would like to receive an autographed copy of this book or other books published by the author, please email the following information to info@openpagespublishing.com:

- Full Name
- Address (street address, city, state, zip, country)
- Phone Number (including area code)
- Indicate which book(s) you are interested in. For a list: www.my411books.com
- Name of the person the book should be autographed to
- Indicate if for a special occasion (birthday, anniversary, graduation)
- You will be contacted with payment information. Payment methods include Visa, MasterCard, Discover, American Express, and PayPal.

_____VISIT MY411BOOKS.COM_____

www.ingramcontent.com/pod-product-compliance
Lightning Source LLC
LaVergne TN
LVHW021502080426
835509LV00018B/2370

*9 780996 068796*